SELECTED
POETRY OF
W. H. AUDEN

SECOND EDITION

SELECTED
POETRY OF
W. H. AUDEN

SECOND EDITION

Chosen for this edition by the author

VINTAGE BOOKS

A Division of Random House
New York

"Metalogue To The Magic Flute"
appeared first in Harper's Bazaar.
The following poems appeared
originally in The New Yorker:
"On the Circuit," "Thanksgiving for a Habitat,"
"Grub First, Then Ethics,"
"After Reading a Child's Guide to Modern Physics,"
and "The Horatians."

ISBN: 0–394–71102–5
Library of Congress Catalog Card Number: 59–5907
Manufactured in the United States of America

First Vintage Books Edition September, 1971

CONTENTS

SELECTED
POETRY OF
W. H. AUDEN

SECOND EDITION

THE LETTER

From the very first coming down
Into a new valley with a frown
Because of the sun and a lost way,
You certainly remain: to-day
I, crouching behind a sheep-pen, heard
Travel across a sudden bird,
Cry out against the storm, and found
The year's arc a completed round
And love's worn circuit re-begun,
Endless with no dissenting turn.
Shall see, shall pass, as we have seen
The swallow on the tile, spring's green
Preliminary shiver, passed
A solitary truck, the last
Of shunting in the Autumn. But now,
To interrupt the homely brow,
Thought warmed to evening through and through,
Your letter comes, speaking as you,
Speaking of much but not to come.

Nor speech is close nor fingers numb
If love not seldom has received
An unjust answer, was deceived.
I, decent with the seasons, move,
Different or with a different love,
Nor question overmuch the nod,
The stone smile of this country god
That never was more reticent,
Always afraid to say more than it meant.

3

TALLER TO-DAY

Taller to-day, we remember similar evenings,
Walking together in a windless orchard
Where the brook runs over the gravel, far from the glacier.

Nights come bringing the snow, and the dead howl
Under headlands in their windy dwelling
Because the Adversary put too easy questions
On lonely roads.

But happy now, though no nearer each other,
We see farms lighted all along the valley;
Down at the mill-shed hammering stops
And men go home.

Noises at dawn will bring
Freedom for some, but not this peace
No bird can contradict: passing, but is sufficient now
For something fulfilled this hour, loved or endured.

THE JOURNEY

To throw away the key and walk away,
Not abrupt exile, the neighbours asking why,
But following a line with left and right,
An altered gradient at another rate,
Learns more than maps upon the whitewashed wall,
The hand put up to ask; and makes us well
Without confession of the ill. All pasts
Are single old past now, although some posts
Are forwarded, held looking on a new view;

The future shall fulfil a surer vow.
Not smiling at queen over the glass rim
Nor making gunpowder in the top room,
Not swooping at the surface still like gulls
But with prolonged drowning shall develop gills.
But there are still to tempt; areas not seen
Because of blizzards or an erring sign
Whose guessed at wonders would be worth alleging,
And lies about the cost of a night's lodging;
Travellers may sleep at inns but not attach;
They sleep one night together, not asked to touch,
Receive no normal welcome, not the pressed lip,
Children to lift, not the assuaging lap,
Crossing the pass descend the growing stream
Too tired to hear except the pulses' strum,
Reach villages to ask for a bed in,
Rock shutting out the sky, the old life done.

NO CHANGE OF PLACE

Who will endure
Heat of day and winter danger,
Journey from one place to another,
Nor be content to lie
Till evening upon headland over bay,
Between the land and sea
Or smoking wait till hour of food,
Leaning on chained-up gate
At edge of wood?

Metals run,
Burnished or rusty in the sun,

From town to town,
And signals all along are down;
Yet nothing passes
But envelopes between these places,
Snatched at the gate and panting read indoors,
And first spring flowers arriving smashed,
Disaster stammered over wires,
And pity flashed.

For should professional traveller come,
Asked at the fireside he is dumb,
Declining with a secret smile,
And all the while
Conjectures on our maps grow stranger
And threaten danger.

There is no change of place:
No one will ever know
For what conversion brilliant capital is waiting,
What ugly feast may village band be celebrating;
For no one goes
Further than railhead or the ends of piers,
Will neither go nor send his son
Further through foothills than the rotting stack
Where gaitered gamekeeper with dog and gun
Will shout 'Turn back'.

THE QUESTION

To ask the hard question is simple:
Asking at meeting

With the simple glance of acquaintance
To what these go
And how these do;
To ask the hard question is simple,
The simple act of the confused will.

But the answer
Is hard and hard to remember:
On steps or on shore
The ears listening
To words at meeting,
The eyes looking
At the hands helping,
Are never sure
Of what they learn
From how these things are done,
And forgetting to listen or see
Makes forgetting easy,
Only remembering the method of remembering,
Remembering only in another way,
Only the strangely exciting lie,
Afraid
To remember what the fish ignored,
How the bird escaped, or if the sheep obeyed.

Till, losing memory,
Bird, fish, and sheep are ghostly,
And ghosts must do again
What gives them pain.
Cowardice cries
For windy skies,
Coldness for water,
Obedience for a master.

Shall memory restore
The steps and the shore,
The face and the meeting place;
Shall the bird live,

Shall the fish dive,
And sheep obey
In a sheep's way;
Can love remember
The question and the answer,
For love recover
What has been dark and rich and warm all over?

THIS LUNAR BEAUTY

This lunar beauty
Has no history,
Is complete and early;
If beauty later
Bear any feature
It had a lover
And is another.

This like a dream
Keeps other time,
And daytime is
The loss of this;
For time is inches
And the heart's changes
Where ghost has haunted,
Lost and wanted.

But this was never
A ghost's endeavour
Nor, finished this,

Was ghost at ease;
And till it pass
Love shall not near
The sweetness here
Nor sorrow take
His endless look.

THIS ONE

Before this loved one
Was that one and that one
A family
And history
And ghost's adversity
Whose pleasing name
Was neighbourly shame.
Before this last one
Was much to be done,
Frontiers to cross
As clothes grew worse
And coins to pass
In a cheaper house
Before this last one
Before this loved one.

Face that the sun
Is supple on
May stir but here
Is no new year;
This gratitude for gifts is less

Than the old loss;
Touching is shaking hands
On mortgaged lands;
And smiling of
This gracious greeting
'Good day. Good luck'
Is no real meeting
But instinctive look
A backward love.

CHORUS

Doom is dark and deeper than any sea-dingle.
Upon what man it fall
In spring, day-wishing flowers appearing,
Avalanche sliding, white snow from rock-face,
That he should leave his house,
No cloud-soft hand can hold him, restraint by women;
But ever that man goes
Through place-keepers, through forest trees,
A stranger to strangers over undried sea,
Houses for fishes, suffocating water,
Or lonely on fell as chat,
By pot-holed becks
A bird stone-haunting, an unquiet bird.

There head falls forward, fatigued at evening,
And dreams of home,
Waving from window, spread of welcome,
Kissing of wife under single sheet;

But waking sees
Bird-flocks nameless to him, through doorway voices
Of new men making another love.

Save him from hostile capture,
From sudden tiger's spring at corner;
Protect his house,
His anxious house where days are counted
From thunderbolt protect,
From gradual ruin spreading like a stain;
Converting number from vague to certain,
Bring joy, bring day of his returning,
Lucky with day approaching, with leaning dawn.

THE WATCHERS

Now from my window-sill I watch the night,
The church clock's yellow face, the green pier light
Burn for a new imprudent year;
The silence buzzes in my ear;
The lights of near-by families are out.

Under the darkness nothing seems to stir;
The lilac bush like a conspirator
Shams dead upon the lawn, and there
Above the flagstaff the Great Bear
Hangs as a portent over Helensburgh.

O Lords of Limit, training dark and light
And setting a tabu 'twixt left and right,

The influential quiet twins
From whom all property begins,
Look leniently upon us all to-night.

No one has seen you: none can say; 'Of late—
Here. You can see the marks—They lay in wait,'
But in my thoughts to-night you seem
Forms which I saw once in a dream,
The stocky keepers of a wild estate.

With guns beneath your arms, in sun and wet,
At doorways posted or on ridges set,
By copse or bridge we know you there
Whose sleepless presences endear
Our peace to us with a perpetual threat.

Look not too closely, be not over-quick;
We have no invitation, but we are sick,
Using the mole's device, the carriage
Of peacock or rat's desperate courage,
And we shall only pass you by a trick.

Deeper towards the summer the year moves on.
What if the starving visionary have seen
The carnival within our gates,
Your bodies kicked about the streets,
We need your power still: use it, that none,

O, from their tables break uncontrollably away,
Lunging, insensible to injury,
Dangerous in a room or out wild-
-ly spinning like a top in through the field,
Mopping and mowing through the sleepless day.

ODE

Though aware of our rank and alert to obey orders,
Watching with binoculars the movement of the grass for an
    ambush,
The pistol cocked, the code-word committed to memory;
         The youngest drummer
Knows all the peace-time stories like the oldest soldier,
         Though frontier-conscious.

About the tall white gods who landed from their open boat,
Skilled in the working of copper, appointing our feast-days,
Before the islands were submerged, when the weather was
    calm,
         The maned lion common,
An open wishing-well in every garden;
         When love came easy.

Certain, all of us, of what happened but not from the records,
Not from the unshaven agent who returned to the camp;
The pillar dug from the desert recorded only
         The sack of a city,
The agent clutching his side collapsed at our feet,
         'Sorry! They got me!'

Yes, they were living here once but do not now,
Yes, they are living still but do not here;
Lying awake after Lights Out a recruit may speak up:
         'Who told you all this?'
The tent-talk pauses a little till a veteran answers
         'Go to sleep, Sonny!'

Turning over he closes his eyes, and then in a moment
Sees the sun at midnight bright over cornfield and pasture,
Our hope . . . Someone jostles him, fumbling for boots,
         Time to change guard:
Boy, the quarrel was before your time, the aggressor
         No one you know.

Your childish moments of awareness were all of our world,
At five you sprang, already a tiger in the garden,
At night your mother taught you to pray for our Daddy
Far away fighting,
One morning you fell off a horse and your brother mocked
you:
'Just like a girl!'

Now we're due to parade on the square in front of the
Cathedral,
When the bishop has blessed us, to file in after the choir-boys,
To stand with the wine-dark conquerors in the roped-off pews,
Shout ourselves hoarse:
'They ran like hares; we have broken them up like firewood;
They fought against God.'

While in a great rift in the limestone miles away
At the same hour they gather, tethering their horses beside
them;
A scarecrow prophet from a boulder foresees our judgment,
Their oppressors howling;
And the bitter psalm is caught by the gale from the rocks:
'How long shall they flourish?'

What have we all been doing to have made from Fear
That laconic war-bitten captain addressing them now?
'Heart and head shall be keener, mood the more
As our might lessens':
To have caused their shout 'We will fight till we lie down beside
The Lord we have loved.'

There's Wrath who has learnt every trick of guerrilla warfare,
The shamming dead, the night-raid, the feinted retreat;
Envy their brilliant pamphleteer, to lying
As husband true,
Expert impersonator and linguist, proud of his power
To hoodwink sentries.

Gluttony living alone, austerer than us,
Quiet Avarice, Acedia famed with them all
For her stamina, keeping the outposts, and somewhere Lust
        With his sapper's skill,
Muttering to his fuses in a tunnel 'Could I meet here with Love,
        I would hug her to death.'

There are faces there for which for a very long time
We've been on the look-out, though often at home we
    imagined,
Catching sight of a back or hearing a voice through a doorway,
        We had found them at last;
Put our arms round their necks and looked in their eyes and
    discovered
        We were unlucky.

And some of them, surely, we seem to have seen before:
Why, that girl who rode off on her bicycle one fine summer
        evening
And never returned, she's there; and the banker we'd noticed
        Worried for weeks;
Till he failed to arrive one morning and his room was empty,
        Gone with a suitcase.

They speak of things done on the frontier we were never told,
The hidden path to their squat Pictish tower
They will never reveal though kept without sleep, for their code
    is
        'Death to the squealer';
They are brave, yes, though our newspapers mention their
    bravery
        In inverted commas.

But careful; back to our lines; it is unsafe there,
Passports are issued no longer; that area is closed;
There's no fire in the waiting-room now at the climbers'
    Junction,
        And all this year

Work has been stopped on the power-house; the wind whistles
    under
             The half-built culverts.

All leave is cancelled to-night; we must say good-bye.
We entrain at once for the North; we shall see in the morning
The headlands we're doomed to attack; snow down to the tide-
    line:
             Though the bunting signals
'Indoors before it's too late; cut peat for your fires,'
             We shall lie out there.

THE DECOYS

There are some birds in these valleys
Who flutter round the careless
With intimate appeal,
By seeming kindness trained to snaring,
They feel no falseness.

Under the spell completely
They circle can serenely,
And in the tricky light
The masked hill has a purer greenness.
Their flight looks fleeter.

Alas, the signal given.
Fingers on trigger tighten.
The real unlucky dove
Must smarting fall away from brightness,
Its love from living.

THE THREE COMPANIONS

'O where are you going?' said reader to rider,
'That valley is fatal when furnaces burn,
Yonder's the midden whose odours will madden,
That gap is the grave where the tall return.'

'O do you imagine,' said fearer to farer,
'That dusk will delay on your path to the pass,
Your diligent looking discover the lacking
Your footsteps feel from granite to grass?'

'O what was that bird,' said horror to hearer,
'Did you see that shape in the twisted trees?
Behind you swiftly the figure comes softly,
The spot on your skin is a shocking disease?'

'Out of this house'—said rider to reader,
'Yours never will'—said farer to fearer,
'They're looking for you'—said hearer to horror,
As he left them there, as he left them there.

IN LEGEND

Enter with him
These legends, Love;
For him assume
Each diverse form
To legend native,
As legend queer;

That he may do
What these require,
Be, Love, like him
To legend true.

When he to ease
His heart's disease
Must cross in sorrow
Corrosive seas,
As dolphin go;
As cunning fox
Guide through the rocks,
Tell in his ear
The common phrase
Required to please
The guardians there;
And when across
The livid marsh
Big birds pursue,
Again be true,
Between his thighs
As pony rise,
And swift as wind
Bear him away
Till cries and they
Are left behind.

But when at last,
These dangers passed,
His grown desire
Of legend tire,
O then, Love, standing
At legend's ending,
Claim your reward;
Submit your neck
To the ungrateful stroke
Of his reluctant sword,
That, starting back,

His eyes may look
Amazed on you,
Find what he wanted
Is faithful too
But disenchanted,
Your human love.

THE QUARRY

O what is that sound which so thrills the ear
 Down in the valley drumming, drumming?
Only the scarlet soldiers, dear,
 The soldiers coming.

O what is that light I see flashing so clear
 Over the distance brightly, brightly?
Only the sun on their weapons, dear,
 As they step lightly.

O what are they doing with all that gear,
 What are they doing this morning, this morning?
Only their usual manoeuvres, dear,
 Or perhaps a warning.

O why have they left the road down there,
 Why are they suddenly wheeling, wheeling?
Perhaps a change in their orders, dear.
 Why are you kneeling?

O haven't they stopped for the doctor's care,
 Haven't they reined their horses, their horses?

Why, they are none of them wounded, dear,
    None of these forces.

O is it the parson they want, with white hair,
    Is it the parson, is it, is it?
No, they are passing his gateway, dear,
    Without a visit.

O it must be the farmer who lives so near.
    It must be the farmer so cunning, so cunning?
They have passed the farmyard already, dear,
    And now they are running.

O where are you going? Stay with me here!
    Were the vows you swore deceiving, deceiving?
No, I promised to love you, dear,
    But I must be leaving.

O it's broken the lock and splintered the door,
    O it's the gate where they're turning, turning;
Their boots are heavy on the floor
    And their eyes are burning.

SEASCAPE

Look, stranger, on this island now
The leaping light for your delight discovers,
Stand stable here
And silent be,
That through the channels of the ear

May wander like a river
The swaying sound of the sea.

Here at a small field's ending pause
When the chalk wall falls to the foam and its tall ledges
Oppose the pluck
And knock of the tide,
And the shingle scrambles after the suck-
-ing surf,
And a gull lodges
A moment on its sheer side.

Far off like floating seeds the ships
Diverge on urgent voluntary errands,
And this full view
Indeed may enter
And move in memory as now these clouds do,
That pass the harbour mirror
And all the summer through the water saunter.

A DREAM

Dear, though the night is gone,
Its dream still haunts today,
That brought us to a room
Cavernous, lofty as
A railway terminus,
And crowded in that gloom
Were beds, and we in one
In a far corner lay.

Our whisper woke no clocks,
We kissed and I was glad
At everything you did,
Indifferent to those
Who sat with hostile eyes
In pairs on every bed,
Arms round each other's neck,
Inert and vaguely sad.

What buried worm of guilt
Or what malignant doubt
Am I the victim of,
That you then, unabashed,
Did what I never wished,
Confessed another love;
And I, submissive, felt
Unwanted and went out?

SONG

—'O for doors to be open and an invite with gilded edges
    To dine with Lord Lobcock and Count Asthma on the
        platinum benches,
    With somersaults and fireworks, the roast and the smacking
        kisses'—
               Cried the cripples to the silent statue,
               The six beggared cripples.

—'And Garbo's and Cleopatra's wits to go astraying,
    In a feather ocean with me to go fishing and playing,
    Still jolly when the cock has burst himself with crowing—

Cried the cripples to the silent statue,
The six beggared cripples.

—'And to stand on green turf among the craning yellow faces
Dependent on the chestnut, the sable, and Arabian horses,
And me with a magic crystal to foresee their places'—
Cried the cripples to the silent statue,
The six beggared cripples.

—'And this square to be deck and these pigeons sails to rig,
And to follow the delicious breeze like a tantony pig
To the shaded feverless islands where the melons are big'—
Cried the cripples to the silent statue,
The six beggared cripples.

—'And these shops to be turned to tulips in a garden bed,
And me with my crutch to thrash each merchant dead
As he pokes from a flower his bald and wicked head'—
Cried the cripples to the silent statue,
The six beggared cripples.

—'And a hole in the bottom of heaven, and Peter and Paul
And each smug surprised saint like parachutes to fall,
And every one-legged beggar to have no legs at all'—
Cried the cripples to the silent statue,
The six beggared cripples.

AUTUMN SONG

Now the leaves are falling fast,
Nurse's flowers will not last;

Nurses to their graves are gone,
And the prams go rolling on.

Whispering neighbours, left and right,
Pluck us from our real delight;
And our active hands must freeze
Lonely on our separate knees.

Dead in hundreds at the back
Follow wooden in our track,
Arms raised stiffly to reprove
In false attitudes of love.

Starving through the leafless wood
Trolls run scolding for their food;
And the nightingale is dumb,
And the angel will not come.

Cold, impossible, ahead
Lifts the mountain's lovely head
Whose white waterfall could bless
Travellers in their last distress.

ONE EVENING

As I walked out one evening,
   Walking down Bristol Street,
The crowds upon the pavement
   Were fields of harvest wheat.

And down by the brimming river
  I heard a lover sing
Under an arch of the railway:
  'Love has no ending.

I'll love you, dear, I'll love you
  Till China and Africa meet,
And the river jumps over the mountain
  And the salmon sing in the street.

I'll love you till the ocean
  Is folded and hung up to dry,
And the seven stars go squawking
  Like geese about the sky.

The years shall run like rabbits,
  For in my arms I hold
The Flower of the Ages,
  And the first love of the world.'

But all the clocks in the city
  Began to whirr and chime:
'O let not Time deceive you,
  You cannot conquer Time.

'In the burrows of the Nightmare
  Where Justice naked is,
Time watches from the shadow
  And coughs when you would kiss.

'In headaches and in worry
  Vaguely life leaks away,
And Time will have his fancy
  To-morrow or to-day.

'Into many a green valley
  Drifts the appalling snow;

Time breaks the threaded dances
    And the diver's brilliant bow.

'O plunge your hands in water,
    Plunge them in up to the wrist;
Stare, stare in the basin
    And wonder what you've missed.

'The glacier knocks in the cupboard,
    The desert sighs in the bed,
And the crack in the tea-cup opens
    A lane to the land of the dead.

'Where the beggars raffle the banknotes
    And the Giant is enchanting to Jack,
And the Lily-white Boy is a Roarer,
    And Jill goes down on her back.

'O look, look in the mirror,
    O look in your distress;
Life remains a blessing
    Although you cannot bless.

'O stand, stand at the window
    As the tears scald and start;
You shall love your crooked neighbour
    With your crooked heart'.

It was late, late in the evening
    The lovers they were gone;
The clocks had ceased their chiming,
    And the deep river ran on.

LULLABY

Lay your sleeping head, my love,
Human on my faithless arm;
Time and fevers burn away
Individual beauty from
Thoughtful children, and the grave
Proves the child ephemeral:
But in my arms till break of day
Let the living creature lie,
Mortal, guilty, but to me
The entirely beautiful.

Soul and body have no bounds:
To lovers as they lie upon
Her tolerant enchanted slope
In their ordinary swoon,
Grave the vision Venus sends
Of supernatural sympathy,
Universal love and hope;
While an abstract insight wakes
Among the glaciers and the rocks
The hermit's sensual ecstasy.

Certainty, fidelity
On the stroke of midnight pass
Like vibrations of a bell,
And fashionable madmen raise
Their pedantic boring cry:
Every farthing of the cost,
All the dreaded cards foretell,
Shall be paid, but from this night
Not a whisper, not a thought,
Not a kiss nor look be lost.

Beauty, midnight, vision dies:
Let the winds of dawn that blow
Softly round your dreaming head

Such a day of sweetness show
Eye and knocking heart may bless,
Find the mortal world enough;
Noons of dryness see you fed
By the involuntary powers,
Nights of insult let you pass
Watched by every human love.

UNDERNEATH THE ABJECT WILLOW

Underneath the abject willow,
    Lover, sulk no more:
Act from thought should quickly follow.
    What is thinking for?
Your unique and moping station
    Proves you cold;
    Stand up and fold
Your map of desolation.

Bells that toll across the meadows
    From the sombre spire
Toll for these unloving shadows
    Love does not require.
All that lives may love; why longer
    Bow to loss
    With arms across?
Strike and you shall conquer.

Geese in flocks above you flying
    Their direction know,

Brooks beneath the thin ice flowing
   To their oceans go.
Dark and dull is your distraction,
   Walk then, come,
   No longer numb
Into your satisfaction.

MADRIGAL

O lurcher-loving collier, black as night,
Follow your love across the smokeless hill;
Your lamp is out and all the cages still;
Course for her heart and do not miss,
But Sunday soon is past and, Kate, fly not so fast,
For Monday comes when none may kiss:
Be marble to his soot, and to his black be white.

ABLE AT TIMES TO CRY

Wrapped in a yielding air, beside
   The flower's soundless hunger,
Close to the tree's clandestine tide,

Close to the bird's high fever,
Loud in his hope and anger,
Erect about his skeleton,
Stands the expressive lover,
Stands the deliberate man.

Beneath the hot incurious sun,
Past stronger beasts and fairer
He picks his way, a living gun,
With gun and lens and bible,
A militant enquirer,
The friend, the rash, the enemy,
The essayist, the able,
Able at times to cry.

The friendless and unhated stone
Lies everywhere about him,
The Brothered-One, the Not-Alone,
The bothered and the hated
Whose family have taught him
To set against the large and dumb,
The timeless and the rooted,
His money and his time.

For mother's fading hopes become
Dull wives to his dull spirits
Soon dulled by nurse's moral thumb,
That dullard fond betrayer
And, childish, he inherits,
So soon by legal father tricked,
The tall impressive tower,
Impressive, yes, but locked.

And ruled by dead men never met,
By pious guess deluded,
Upon the stool of madness set
Or stool of desolation,
Sits murderous and clear-headed;

Enormous beauties round him move,
    For grandiose is his vision
    And grandiose his love.

Determined on Time's honest shield
    The lamb must face the tigress,
Their faithful quarrel never healed
    Though, faithless, he consider
    His dream of vaguer ages,
Hunter and victim reconciled,
    The lion and the adder,
    The adder and the child.

Fresh loves betray him, every day
    Over his green horizon
A fresh deserter rides away,
    And miles away birds mutter
    Of ambush and of treason;
To fresh defeats he still must move,
    To further griefs and greater,
    And the defeat of grief.

TWO SONGS FOR HEDLI ANDERSON

I

Stop all the clocks, cut off the telephone,
Prevent the dog from barking with a juicy bone,
Silence the pianos and with muffled drum
Bring out the coffin, let the mourners come.

Let aeroplanes circle moaning overhead
Scribbling on the sky the message He Is Dead,

Put crêpe bows round the white necks of the public doves,
Let the traffic policemen wear black cotton gloves.

He was my North, my South, my East and West,
My working week and my Sunday rest,
My noon, my midnight, my talk, my song;
I thought that love would last for ever: I was wrong.

The stars are not wanted now: put out every one;
Pack up the moon and dismantle the sun;
Pour away the ocean and sweep up the wood.
For nothing now can ever come to any good.

II

O the valley in the summer where I and my John
Beside the deep river would walk on and on
While the flowers at our feet and the birds up above
Argued so sweetly on reciprocal love,
And I leaned on his shoulder; 'O Johnny, let's play':
But he frowned like thunder and he went away.

O that Friday near Christmas as I well recall
When we went to the Charity Matinee Ball,
The floor was so smooth and the band was so loud
And Johnny so handsome I felt so proud;
'Squeeze me tighter, dear Johnny, let's dance till it's day':
But he frowned like thunder and he went away.

Shall I ever forget at the Grand Opera
When music poured out of each wonderful star?
Diamonds and pearls they hung dazzling down
Over each silver or golden silk gown;
'O John I'm in heaven,' I whispered to say:
But he frowned like thunder and he went away.

O but he was as fair as a garden in flower,
As slender and tall as the great Eiffel Tower,
When the waltz throbbed out on the long promenade

O his eyes and his smile they went straight to my heart;
'O marry me, Johnny, I'll love and obey':
But he frowned like thunder and he went away.

O last night I dreamed of you, Johnny, my lover,
You'd the sun on one arm and the moon on the other,
The sea it was blue and the grass it was green,
Every star rattled a round tambourine;
Ten thousand miles deep in a pit there I lay:
But you frowned like thunder and you went away.

MISS GEE. A BALLAD

Let me tell you a little story
    About Miss Edith Gee;
She lived in Clevedon Terrace
    At Number 83.

She'd a slight squint in her left eye,
    Her lips they were thin and small,
She had narrow sloping shoulders
    And she had no bust at all.

She'd a velvet hat with trimmings,
    And a dark grey serge costume;
She lived in Clevedon Terrace
    In a small bed-sitting room.

She'd a purple mac for wet days,
    A green umbrella too to take,

She'd a bicycle with shopping basket
    And a harsh back-pedal brake.

The Church of Saint Aloysius
    Was not so very far;
She did a lot of knitting,
    Knitting for that Church Bazaar.

Miss Gee looked up at the starlight
    And said: 'Does anyone care
That I live in Clevedon Terrace
    On one hundred pounds a year?'

She dreamed a dream one evening
    That she was the Queen of France
And the Vicar of Saint Aloysius
    Asked Her Majesty to dance.

But a storm blew down the palace,
    She was biking through a field of corn,
And a bull with the face of the Vicar
    Was charging with lowered horn.

She could feel his hot breath behind her,
    He was going to overtake;
And the bicycle went slower and slower
    Because of that back-pedal brake.

Summer made the trees a picture,
    Winter made them a wreck;
She bicycled to the evening service
    With her clothes buttoned up to her neck.

She passed by the loving couples,
    She turned her head away;
She passed by the loving couples
    And they didn't ask her to stay.

Miss Gee sat down in the side-aisle,
  She heard the organ play;
And the choir it sang so sweetly
  At the ending of the day,

Miss Gee knelt down in the side-aisle,
  She knelt down on her knees:
'Lead me not into temptation
  But make me a good girl, please.'

The days and nights went by her
  Like waves round a Cornish wreck;
She bicycled down to the doctor
  With her clothes buttoned up to her neck.

She bicycled down to the doctor,
  And rang the surgery bell:
'O, doctor, I've a pain inside me,
  And I don't feel very well.'

Doctor Thomas looked her over,
  And then he looked some more;
Walked over to his wash-basin,
  Said, 'Why didn't you come before?'

Doctor Thomas sat over his dinner,
  Though his wife was waiting to ring;
Rolling his bread into pellets,
  Said, 'Cancer's a funny thing.'

His wife she rang for the servant,
  Said, 'Don't be so morbid, dear.'
He said: 'I saw Miss Gee this evening
  And she's a goner, I fear.'

They took Miss Gee to the hospital,
  She lay there a total wreck,

Lay in the ward for women
　　With the bedclothes right up to her neck.

They laid her on the table,
　　The students began to laugh;
And Mr Rose the surgeon
　　He cut Miss Gee in half.

Mr Rose he turned to his students,
　　Said, 'Gentlemen, if you please,
We seldom see a sarcoma
　　As far advanced as this.'

They took her off the table,
　　They wheeled away Miss Gee
Down to another department
　　Where they study Anatomy.

They hung her from the ceiling,
　　Yes, they hung up Miss Gee;
And a couple of Oxford Groupers
　　Carefully dissected her knee.

ROMAN WALL BLUES

Over the heather the wet wind blows,
I've lice in my tunic and a cold in my nose.

The rain comes pattering out of the sky,
I'm a Wall soldier, I don't know why.

The mist creeps over the hard grey stone,
My girl's in Tungria; I sleep alone.

Aulus goes hanging around her place,
I don't like his manners, I don't like his face.

Piso's a Christian, he worships a fish;
There'd be no kissing if he had his wish.

She gave me a ring but I diced it away;
I want my girl and I want my pay.

When I'm a veteran with only one eye
I shall do nothing but look at the sky.

VICTOR. A BALLAD

Victor was a little baby,
    Into this world he came;
His father took him on his knee and said:
    'Don't dishonour the family name.'

Victor looked up at his father
    Looked up with big round eyes:
His father said; 'Victor, my only son,
    Don't you ever ever tell lies.'

Victor and his father went riding
    Out in a little dog-cart;
His father took a Bible from his pocket and read;
    'Blessed are the pure in heart.'

It was a frosty December
      Victor was only eighteen,
But his figures were neat and his margins straight
      And his cuffs were always clean.

He took a room at the Peveril,
      A respectable boarding-house;
And Time watched Victor day after day
      As a cat will watch a mouse.

The clerks slapped Victor on the shoulder;
      'Have you ever had a woman?' they said,
'Come down town with us on Saturday night.'
      Victor smiled and shook his head.

The manager sat in his office,
      Smoked a Corona cigar:
Said; 'Victor's a decent fellow but
      He's too mousey to go far'.

Victor went up to his bedroom,
      Set the alarum bell;
Climbed into bed, took his Bible and read
      Of what happened to Jezebel.

It was the First of April,
      Anna to the Peveril came;
Her eyes, her lips, her breasts, her hips
      And her smile set men aflame.

She looked as pure as a schoolgirl
      On her First Communion day,
But her kisses were like the best champagne
      When she gave herself away.

It was the Second of April,
      She was wearing a coat of fur;

Victor met her upon the stairs
    And he fell in love with her.

The first time he made his proposal,
    She laughed, said; 'I'll never wed';
The second time there was a pause;
    Then she smiled and shook her head.

Anna looked into her mirror,
    Pouted and gave a frown:
Said; 'Victor's as dull as a wet afternoon
    But I've got to settle down.'

The third time he made his proposal,
    As they walked by the Reservoir:
She gave him a kiss like a blow on the head,
    Said; 'You are my heart's desire.'

They were married early in August,
    She said; 'Kiss me, you funny boy':
Victor took her in his arms and said;
    'O my Helen of Troy.'

It was the middle of September,
    Victor came to the office one day;
He was wearing a flower in his buttonhole,
    He was late but he was gay.

The clerks were talking of Anna,
    The door was just ajar:
One said; 'Poor old Victor, but where ignorance
    Is bliss, et cetera.'

Victor stood still as a statue,
    The door was just ajar:
One said; 'God, what fun I had with her
    In that Baby Austin car.'

Victor walked out into the High Street,
    He walked to the edge of the town;
He came to the allotments and the rubbish heap
    And his tears came tumbling down.

Victor looked up at the sunset
    As he stood there all alone;
Cried: 'Are you in Heaven, Father?'
    But the sky said 'Address not known'.

Victor looked up at the mountains,
    The mountains all covered with snow
Cried; 'Are you pleased with me, Father?'
    And the answer came back, No.

Victor came to the forest,
    Cried: 'Father, will she ever be true?'
And the oaks and the beeches shook their heads
    And they answered: 'Not to you.'

Victor came to the meadow
    Where the wind went sweeping by:
Cried; 'O Father, I love her so',
    But the wind said, 'She must die'.

Victor came to the river
    Running so deep and so still:
Crying; 'O Father, what shall I do?'
    And the river answered, 'Kill'.

Anna was sitting at table,
    Drawing cards from a pack;
Anna was sitting at table
    Waiting for her husband to come back.

It wasn't the Jack of Diamonds
    Nor the Joker she drew at first;

It wasn't the King or the Queen of Hearts
    But the Ace of Spades reversed.

Victor stood in the doorway,
    He didn't utter a word:
She said; 'What's the matter, darling?'
    He behaved as if he hadn't heard.

There was a voice in his left ear,
    There was a voice in his right,
There was a voice at the base of his skull
    Saying, 'She must die tonight.'

Victor picked up a carving-knife,
    His features were set and drawn,
Said; 'Anna, it would have been better for you
    If you had not been born.'

Anna jumped up from the table,
    Anna started to scream,
But Victor came slowly after her
    Like a horror in a dream.

She dodged behind the sofa,
    She tore down a curtain rod,
But Victor came slowly after her:
    Said; 'Prepare to meet thy God.'

She managed to wrench the door open,
    She ran and she didn't stop.
But Victor followed her up the stairs
    And he caught her at the top.

He stood there above the body,
    He stood there holding the knife;
And the blood ran down the stairs and sang,
    'I'm the Resurrection and the Life'.

They tapped Victor on the shoulder,
    They took him away in a van;
He sat as quiet as a lump of moss
    Saying, 'I am the Son of Man'.

Victor sat in a corner
    Making a woman of clay:
Saying; 'I am Alpha and Omega, I shall come
    To judge the earth one day.'

[handwritten annotation: Victor's religious mania — caused by father's train...]

THE DEAD ECHO

'O who can ever gaze his fill,'
    Farmer and fisherman say,
'On native shore and local hill,
Grudge aching limb or callus on the hand?
Fathers, grandfathers stood upon this land,
And here the pilgrims from our loins shall stand.'
    So farmer and fisherman say
    In their fortunate heyday:
    But Death's soft answer drifts across
    Empty catch or harvest loss
        Or an unlucky May.
The earth is an oyster with nothing inside it,
    Not to be born is the best for man;
The end of toil is a bailiff's order,
    Throw down the mattock and dance while you can.

'O life's too short for friends who share,'
    Travellers think in their hearts,

42

'The city's common bed, the air,
The mountain bivouac and the bathing beach,
Where incidents draw every day from each
Memorable gesture and witty speech.'
    So travellers think in their hearts,
    Till malice or circumstance parts
    Them from their constant humour:
    And slyly Death's coercive rumour
        In the silence starts.
A friend is the old old tale of Narcissus,
    Not to be born is the best for man;
An active partner in something disgraceful,
    Change your partner, dance while you can.

'O stretch your hands across the sea,'
    The impassioned lover cries,
'Stretch them towards your harm and me.
Our grass is green, and sensual our brief bed,
The stream sings at its foot, and at its head
The mild and vegetarian beasts are fed.'
    So the impassioned lover cries
    Till his storm of pleasure dies:
    From the bedpost and the rocks
    Death's enticing echo mocks,
        And his voice replies.
The greater the love, the more false to its object,
    Not to be born is the best for man;
After the kiss comes the impulse to throttle,
    Break the embraces, dance while you can.

'I see the guilty world forgiven,'
    Dreamer and drunkard sing,
'The ladders let down out of heaven,
The laurels springing from the martyrs' blood,
The children skipping where the weepers stood,
The lovers natural and the beasts all good.'
    So dreamer and drunkard sing
    Till day their sobriety bring:

Parrotwise with death's reply
From whelping fear and nesting lie,
    Woods and their echoes ring.
The desires of the heart are as crooked as corkscrews,
    Not to be born is the best for man;
The second-best is a formal order,
    The dance's pattern; Dance while you can.
Dance, dance, for the figure is easy,
    The tune is catching and will not stop;
Dance till the stars come down with the rafters;
    Dance, dance, dance till you drop.

GANYMEDE

He looked in all His wisdom from the throne
Down on that humble boy who kept the sheep,
And sent a dove; the dove returned alone:
Youth liked the music, but soon fell asleep.

But He had planned such future for the youth:
Surely, His duty now was to compel.
For later he would come to love the truth,
And own his gratitude. His eagle fell.

It did not work. His conversation bored
The boy who yawned and whistled and made faces,
And wriggled free from fatherly embraces;

But with the eagle he was always willing
To go where it suggested, and adored
And learnt from it so many ways of killing.

A NEW AGE

So an age ended, and its last deliverer died
In bed, grown idle and unhappy; they were safe:
The sudden shadow of a giant's enormous calf
Would fall no more at dusk across their lawns outside.

They slept in peace: in marshes here and there no doubt
A sterile dragon lingered to a natural death,
But in a year the spoor had vanished from the heath:
A kobold's knocking in the mountain petered out.

Only the sculptors and the poets were half sad,
And the pert retinue from the magician's house
Grumbled and went elsewhere. The vanquished powers were
    glad

To be invisible and free; without remorse
Struck down the sons who strayed into their course,
And ravished the daughters, and drove the fathers mad.

SURGICAL WARD

They are and suffer; that is all they do;
A bandage hides the place where each is living,
His knowledge of the world restricted to
The treatment that the instruments are giving.

And lie apart like epochs from each other
—Truth in their sense is how much they can bear;

It is not talk like ours, but groans they smother—
And are remote as plants; we stand elsewhere.

For who when healthy can become a foot?
Even a scratch we can't recall when cured,
But are boist'rous in a moment and believe

In the common world of the uninjured, and cannot
Imagine isolation. Only happiness is shared,
And anger, and the idea of love.

EMBASSY

As evening fell the day's oppression lifted;
Far peaks came into focus; it had rained:
Across wide lawns and cultured flowers drifted
The conversation of the highly trained.

Two gardeners watched them pass and priced their shoes:
A chauffeur waited, reading in the drive,
For them to finish their exchange of views;
It seemed a picture of the private life.

Far off, no matter what good they intended,
The armies waited for a verbal error
With all the instruments for causing pain:

And on the issue of their charm depended
A land laid waste, with all its young men slain,
Its women weeping, and its towns in terror.

THE SPHINX

Did it once issue from the carver's hand
Healthy? Even the earliest conquerors saw
The face of a sick ape, a bandaged paw,
A Presence in the hot invaded land.

The lion of a tortured stubborn star,
It does not like the young, nor love, nor learning:
Time hurt it like a person; it lies, turning
A vast behind on shrill America,

And witnesses. The huge hurt face accuses,
And pardons nothing, least of all success.
The answers that it utters have no uses

To those who face akimbo its distress:
'Do people like me?' No. The slave amuses
The lion: 'Am I to suffer always?' Yes.

MACAO

A weed from Catholic Europe, it took root
Between the yellow mountains and the sea,
And bore these gay stone houses like a fruit,
And grew on China imperceptibly.

Rococo images of Saint and Saviour
Promise her gamblers fortunes when they die;

Churches beside the brothels testify
That faith can pardon natural behaviour.

This city of indulgence need not fear
The major sins by which the heart is killed,
And governments and men are torn to pieces:

Religious clocks will strike; the childish vices
Will safeguard the low virtues of the child;
And nothing serious can happen here.

THE BARD

He was their servant—some say he was blind—
And moved among their faces and their things
Their feeling gathered in him like a wind
And sang: they cried—'It is a God that sings'—

And worshipped him and set him up apart
And made him vain till he mistook for song
The little tremors of his mind and heart
At each domestic wrong.

Songs came no more: he had to make them.
With what precision was each strophe planned.
He hugged his sorrow like a plot of land,

And walked like an assassin through the town,
And looked at men and did not like them,
But trembled if one passed him with a frown.

MUSÉE DES BEAUX ARTS

About suffering they were never wrong,
The Old Masters: how well they understood
Its human position; how it takes place
While someone else is eating or opening a window or just
      walking dully along;
How, when the aged are reverently, passionately waiting
For the miraculous birth, there always must be
Children who did not specially want it to happen, skating
On a pond at the edge of the wood:
They never forgot
That even the dreadful martyrdom must run its course
Anyhow in a corner, some untidy spot
Where the dogs go on with their doggy life and the torturer's
      horse
Scratches its innocent behind on a tree.

In Brueghel's *Icarus,* for instance: how everything turns away
Quite leisurely from the disaster; the ploughman may
Have heard the splash, the forsaken cry,
But for him it was not an important failure; the sun shone
As it had to on the white legs disappearing into the green
Water; and the expensive delicate ship that must have seen
Something amazing, a boy falling out of the sky,
Had somewhere to get to and sailed calmly on.

GARE DU MIDI

A nondescript express in from the South,
Crowds round the ticket barrier, a face

To welcome which the mayor has not contrived
Bugles or braid: something about the mouth
Distracts the stray look with alarm and pity.
Snow is falling. Clutching a little case,
He walks out briskly to infect a city
Whose terrible future may have just arrived.

RIMBAUD

The nights, the railway-arches, the bad sky,
His horrible companions did not know it;
But in that child the rhetorician's lie
Burst like a pipe: the cold had made a poet.

Drinks bought him by his weak and lyric friend   *Baudelaire ?*
His senses systematically deranged,
To all accustomed nonsense put an end;
Till he from lyre and weakness was estranged.

Verse was a special illness of the ear;
Integrity was not enough; that seemed
The hell of childhood: he must try again.   *after re-birth*

Now, galloping through Africa, he dreamed
Of a new self, a son, an engineer,
His truth acceptable to lying men.

THE CAPITAL

Quarter of pleasures where the rich are always waiting,
Waiting expensively for miracles to happen,
Dim-lighted restaurant where lovers eat each other,
Café where exiles have established a malicious village:

You with your charm and your apparatus have abolished
The strictness of winter and the spring's compulsion;
Far from your lights the outraged punitive father,
The dullness of mere obedience here is apparent.

So with orchestras and glances, soon you betray us
To belief in our infinite powers; and the innocent
Unobservant offender falls in a moment
Victim to his heart's invisible furies.

In unlighted streets you hide away the appalling;
Factories where lives are made for a temporary use
Like collars or chairs, rooms where the lonely are battered
Slowly like pebbles into fortuitous shapes.

But the sky you illumine, your glow is visible far
Into the dark countryside, the enormous, the frozen,
Where, hinting at the forbidden like a wicked uncle,
Night after night to the farmer's children you beckon.

EPITAPH ON A TYRANT

Perfection, of a kind, was what he was after,
And the poetry he invented was easy to understand;

He knew human folly like the back of his hand,
And was greatly interested in armies and fleets;
When he laughed, respectable senators burst with laughter,
And when he cried the little children died in the streets.

IN MEMORY OF W. B. YEATS

(d. Jan. 1939   d. = Died, or departed

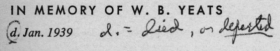

I

He disappeared in the dead of winter:
The brooks were frozen, the airports almost deserted,
And snow disfigured the public statues;
The mercury sank in the mouth of the dying day.
What instruments we have agree
The day of his death was a dark cold day.

Far from his illness
The wolves ran on through the evergreen forests,
The peasant river was untempted by the fashionable quays;
By mourning tongues
The death of the poet was kept from his poems.

But for him it was his last afternoon as himself,
An afternoon of nurses and rumours;
The provinces of his body revolted,
The squares of his mind were empty,
Silence invaded the suburbs,
The current of his feeling failed; he became his admirers.

Now he is scattered among a hundred cities
And wholly given over to unfamiliar affections;

To find his happiness in another kind of wood
And be punished under a foreign code of conscience.
The words of a dead man
Are modified in the guts of the living.

But in the importance and noise of to-morrow
When the brokers are roaring like beasts on the floor of the
    Bourse,
And the poor have the sufferings to which they are fairly
    accustomed,
And each in the cell of himself is almost convinced of his
    freedom,
A few thousand will think of this day
As one thinks of a day when one did something slightly
    unusual.
What instruments we have agree
The day of his death was a dark cold day.

II

You were silly like us; your gift survived it all;
The parish of rich women, physical decay,
Yourself: mad Ireland hurt you into poetry.
Now Ireland has her madness and her weather still,
For poetry makes nothing happen: it survives
In the valley of its saying where executives
Would never want to tamper; it flows south
From ranches of isolation and the busy griefs,
Raw towns that we believe and die in; it survives,
A way of happening, a mouth.

III

Earth, receive an honoured guest:
William Yeats is laid to rest.
Let the Irish vessel lie
Emptied of its poetry.

In the nightmare of the dark
All the dogs of Europe bark,

And the living nations wait,
Each sequestered in its hate;

Intellectual disgrace
Stares from every human face,
And the seas of pity lie
Locked and frozen in each eye.

Follow, poet, follow right
To the bottom of the night,
With your unconstraining voice
Still persuade us to rejoice;

With the farming of a verse
Make a vineyard of the curse,
Sing of human unsuccess
In a rapture of distress;

In the deserts of the heart
Let the healing fountain start,
In the prison of his days
Teach the free man how to praise.

IN MEMORY OF SIGMUND FREUD

d. September 1939

When there are so many we shall have to mourn,
When grief has been made so public, and exposed
      To the critique of a whole epoch
        The frailty of our conscience and anguish,

Of whom shall we speak? For every day they die
Among us, those who were doing us some good,
          And knew it was never enough but
          Hoped to improve a little by living.

Such was this doctor: still at eighty he wished
To think of our life, from whose unruliness
          So many plausible young futures
          With threats or flattery ask obedience.

But his wish was denied him; he closed his eyes
Upon that last picture common to us all,
          Of problems like relatives standing
          Puzzled and jealous about our dying.

For about him at the very end were still
Those he had studied, the nervous and the nights,
          And shades that still waited to enter
          The bright circle of his recognition

Turned elsewhere with their disappointment as he
Was taken away from his old interest
          To go back to the earth in London,
          An important Jew who died in exile.

Only Hate was happy, hoping to augment
His practice now, and his shabby clientèle
          Who think they can be cured by killing
          And covering the gardens with ashes.

They are still alive but in a world he changed
Simply by looking back with no false regrets;
          All that he did was to remember
          Like the old and be honest like children.

He wasn't clever at all: he merely told
The unhappy Present to recite the Past

Like a poetry lesson till sooner
Or later it faltered at the line where

Long ago the accusations had begun,
And suddenly knew by whom it had been judged,
How rich life had been and how silly,
And was life-forgiven and more humble.

Able to approach the Future as a friend
Without a wardrobe of excuses, without
A set mask of rectitude or an
Embarrassing over-familiar gesture.

No wonder the ancient cultures of conceit
In his technique of unsettlement foresaw
The fall of princes, the collapse of
Their lucrative patterns of frustration.

If he succeeded, why, the Generalised Life
Would become impossible, the monolith
Of State be broken and prevented
The co-operation of avengers.

Of course they called on God; but he went his way,
Down among the Lost People like Dante, down
To the stinking fosse where the injured
Lead the ugly life of the rejected.

And showed us what evil is: not, as we thought,
Deeds that must be punished, but our lack of faith,
Our dishonest mood of denial,
The concupiscence of the oppressor.

And if something of the autocratic pose,
The paternal strictness he distrusted, still
Clung to his utterance and features,
It was a protective imitation

For one who lived among enemies so long;
If often he was wrong and at times absurd,
        To us he is no more a person
        Now but a whole climate of opinion,

Under whom we conduct our differing lives;
Like weather he can only hinder or help,
        The proud can still be proud but find it
        A little harder, and the tyrant tries

To make him do but doesn't care for him much.
He quietly surrounds all our habits of growth;
        He extends, till the tired in even
        The remotest most miserable duchy

Have felt the change in their bones and are cheered,
And the child unlucky in his little State,
        Some hearth where freedom is excluded,
        A hive whose honey is fear and worry,

Feels calmer now and somehow assured of escape;
While as they lie in the grass of our neglect,
        So many long-forgotten objects
        Revealed by his undiscouraged shining

Are returned to us and made precious again;
Games we had thought we must drop as we grew up,
        Little noises we dared not laugh at,
        Faces we made when no one was looking.

But he wishes us more than this: to be free
Is often to be lonely; he would unite
        The unequal moieties fractured
        By our own well-meaning sense of justice.

Would restore to the larger the wit and will
The smaller possesses but can only use

For arid disputes, would give back to
The son the mother's richness of feeling.

But he would have us remember most of all
To be enthusiastic over the night
        Not only for the sense of wonder
        It alone has to offer, but also

Because it needs our love: for with sad eyes
Its delectable creatures look up and beg
        Us dumbly to ask them to follow;
        They are exiles who long for the future

That lies in our power. They too would rejoice
If allowed to serve enlightenment like him,
        Even to bear our cry of 'Judas,'
        As he did and all must bear who serve it.

One rational voice is dumb; over a grave
The household of Impulse mourns one dearly loved.
        Sad is Eros, builder of cities,
        And weeping anarchic Aphrodite.

THE QUEST

I

All had been ordered weeks before the start
From the best firms at such work; instruments
To take the measure of all queer events,
And drugs to move the bowels or the heart.

A watch, of course, to watch impatience fly,
Lamps for the dark and shades against the sun;
Foreboding, too, insisted on a gun,
And coloured beads to soothe a savage eye.

In theory they were sound on Expectation
Had there been situations to be in.
Unluckily they were their situation:

One should not give a poisoner medicine,
A conjurer fine apparatus, nor
A rifle to a melancholic bore.

II

Two friends who met here and embraced are gone,
Each to his own mistake; one flashes on
To fame and ruin in a rowdy lie,
A village torpor holds the other one,
Some local wrong where it takes time to die:
This empty junction glitters in the sun.

So at all quays and crossroads: who can tell
These places of decision and farewell,
To what dishonour all adventure leads,
What parting gift could give that friend protection,
So orientated his salvation needs
The Bad Lands and the sinister direction?

All landscapes and all weathers freeze with fear,
But none have ever thought, the legends say,
The time allowed made it impossible;
For even the most pessimistic set
The limit of their errors at a year.
What friends could there be left then to betray,
What joy take longer to atone for; yet
Who would complete without the extra day
The journey that should take no time at all?

III

They noticed that virginity was needed
To trap the unicorn in every case,
But not that, of those virgins who succeeded,
A high percentage had an ugly face.

The hero was as daring as they thought him,
But his peculiar boyhood missed them all;
The angel of a broken leg had taught him
The right precautions to avoid a fall.

So in presumption they set forth alone
On what, for them, was not compulsory
And stuck half-way to settle in some cave
With desert lions to domesticity;

Or turned aside to be absurdly brave,
And met the ogre and were turned to stone.

IV

Incredulous, he stared at the amused
Official writing down his name among
Those whose request to suffer was refused.

The pen ceased scratching; though he came too late
To join the martyrs, there was still a place
Among the tempters for a caustic tongue

To test the resolution of the young
With tales of the small failings of the great,
And shame the eager with ironic praise.

Though mirrors might be hateful for a while
Women and books should teach his middle age
The fencing wit of an informal style

To keep the silences at bay and cage
His pacing manias in a worldly smile.

V

The over-logical fell for the witch
Whose argument converted him to stone;
Thieves rapidly absorbed the over-rich;
The over-popular went mad alone,
And kisses brutalised the over-male.

As agents their effectiveness soon ceased;
Yet, in proportion as they seemed to fail,
Their instrumental value was increased
To those still able to obey their wish.

By standing stones the blind can feel their way,
Wild dogs compel the cowardly to fight,
Beggars assist the slow to travel light,
And even madmen manage to convey
Unwelcome truths in lonely gibberish.

VI

Suppose he'd listened to the erudite committee,
He would have only found where not to look;
Suppose his terrier when he whistled had obeyed,
It would not have unearthed the buried city;
Suppose he had dismissed the careless maid,
The cryptogram would not have fluttered from the book.

'I was not I,' he cried as, healthy and astounded,
He stepped across a predecessor's skull;
'A nonsense jingle simply came into my head
And left the intellectual Sphinx dumbfounded;
I won the Queen because my hair was red;
The terrible adventure is a little dull.'

Hence Failure's torment: 'Was I doomed in any case,
Or would I not have failed had I believed in Grace?'

Fresh addenda are published every day
To the encyclopedia of the Way.

Linguistic notes and scientific explanations,
And texts for schools, with modernized spelling and
    illustrations.

Now everyone knows the hero must choose the old horse,
Abstain from liquor and sexual intercourse

And look out for a stranded fish to be kind to:
Now everyone thinks he could find, had he a mind to,

The way through the waste to the chapel in the rock
For a vision of the Triple Rainbow or the Astral Clock.

Forgetting his information comes mostly from married men
Who liked fishing and a flutter on the horses now and then.

And how reliable can any truth be that is got
By observing oneself and then just inserting a Not?

LAW LIKE LOVE

Law, say the gardeners, is the sun,
Law is the one
All gardeners obey
To-morrow, yesterday, to-day.

Law is the wisdom of the old,
The impotent grandfathers shrilly scold;
The grandchildren put out a treble tongue,
Law is the senses of the young.

Law, says the priest with a priestly look,
Expounding to an unpriestly people,
Law is the words in my priestly book,
Law is my pulpit and my steeple.

Law, says the judge as he looks down his nose,
Speaking clearly and most severely,
Law is as I've told you before,
Law is as you know I suppose,
Law is but let me explain it once more,
Law is The Law.

Yet law-abiding scholars write:
Law is neither wrong nor right,
Law is only crimes
Punished by places and by times,
Law is the clothes men wear
Anytime, anywhere,
Law is Good morning and Good night.

Others say, Law is our Fate;
Others say, Law is our State;
Others say, others say
Law is no more
Law has gone away.

And always the loud angry crowd
Very angry and very loud
Law is We,
And always the soft idiot softly Me.

If we, dear, know we know no more
Than they about the law,

If I no more than you
Know what we should and should not do
Except that all agree
Gladly or miserably
That the law is
And that all know this,
If therefore thinking it absurd
To identify Law with some other word,
Unlike so many men
I cannot say Law is again,
No more than they can we suppress
The universal wish to guess
Or slip out of our own position
Into an unconcerned condition.
Although I can at least confine
Your vanity and mine
To stating timidly
A timid similarity,
We shall boast anyway:
Like love I say.

Like love we don't know where or why
Like love we can't compel or fly
Like love we often weep
Like love we seldom keep.

ANOTHER TIME

For us like any other fugitive,
Like the numberless flowers that cannot number

And all the beasts that need not remember,
It is to-day in which we live.

So many try to say Not Now,
So many have forgotten how
To say I Am, and would be
Lost, if they could, in history.

Bowing, for instance, with such old-world grace
To a proper flag in a proper place,
Muttering like ancients as they stump upstairs
Of Mine and His or Ours and Theirs.

Just as if time were what they used to will
When it was gifted with possession still,
Just as if they were wrong
In no more wishing to belong.

No wonder then so many die of grief,
So many are so lonely as they die;
No one has yet believed or liked a lie,
Another time has other lives to live.

OUR BIAS

The hour-glass whispers to the lion's roar,
The clock-towers tell the gardens day and night,
How many errors Time has patience for,
How wrong they are in being always right.

Yet Time, however loud its chimes or deep,
However fast its falling torrent flows,
Has never put one lion off his leap
Nor shaken the assurance of a rose.

For they, it seems, care only for success:
While we choose words according to their sound
And judge a problem by its awkwardness;

And Time with us was always popular.
When have we not preferred some going round
To going straight to where we are?

HELL

Hell is neither here nor there
Hell is not anywhere
Hell is hard to bear.

It is so hard to dream posterity
Or haunt a ruined century
And so much easier to be.

Only the challenge to our will,
Our pride in learning any skill,
Sustains our effort to be ill.

To talk the dictionary through
Without a chance word coming true
Is more than Darwin's apes could do.

Yet pride alone could not insist
Did we not hope, if we persist,
That one day Hell might actually exist.

In time, pretending to be blind
And universally unkind
Might really send us out of our mind.

If we were really wretched and asleep
It would be then *de trop* to weep,
It would be natural to lie,
There'd be no living left to die.

SONG

Warm are the still and lucky miles,
White shores of longing stretch away,
A light of recognition fills
    The whole great day, and bright
The tiny world of lovers' arms.

Silence invades the breathing wood
Where drowsy limbs a treasure keep,
Now greenly falls in learned shade
    Across the sleeping brows
And stirs their secret to a smile.

Restored! Returned! The lost are born
On seas of shipwreck home at last:

See! In the fire of praising burns
     The dry dumb past, and we
The life-day long shall part no more.

LADY, WEEPING AT THE CROSSROADS

Lady, weeping at the crossroads
Would you meet your love
In the twilight with his greyhounds,
And the hawk on his glove?

Bribe the birds then on the branches.
Bribe them to be dumb,
Stare the hot sun out of heaven
That the night may come.

Starless are the nights of travel,
Bleak the winter wind;
Run with terror all before you
And regret behind.

Run until you hear the ocean's
Everlasting cry;
Deep though it may be and bitter
You must drink it dry.

Wear out patience in the lowest
Dungeons of the sea,
Searching through the stranded shipwrecks
For the golden key.

Push on to the world's end, pay the
Dread guard with a kiss;
Cross the rotten bridge that totters
Over the abyss.

There stands the deserted castle
Ready to explore;
Enter, climb the marble staircase
Open the locked door.

Cross the silent empty ballroom,
Doubt and danger past;
Blow the cobwebs from the mirror
See yourself at last.

Put your hand behind the wainscot,
You have done your part;
Find the penknife there and plunge it
Into your false heart.

IF I COULD TELL YOU

Time will say nothing but I told you so,
Time only knows the price we have to pay;
If I could tell you I would let you know.

If we should weep when clowns put on their show,
If we should stumble when musicians play,
Time will say nothing but I told you so.

There are no fortunes to be told, although,
Because I love you more than I can say,
If I could tell you I would let you know.

The winds must come from somewhere when they blow,
There must be reasons why the leaves decay;
Time will say nothing but I told you so.

Perhaps the roses really want to grow,
The vision seriously intends to stay;
If I could tell you I would let you know.

Suppose the lions all get up and go,
And all the brooks and soldiers run away;
Will Time say nothing but I told you so?
If I could tell you I would let you know.

THE MODEL

Generally, reading palms or handwriting or faces
   Is a job of translation, since the kind
      Gentleman often is
   A seducer, the frowning schoolgirl may
      By dying to be asked to stay;
But the body of this old lady exactly indicates her mind;

Rorschach or Binet could not add to what a fool can see
   From the plain fact that she is alive and well;
      For when one is eighty

Even a teeny-weeny bit of greed
    Makes one very ill indeed,
And a touch of despair is instantaneously fatal:

Whether the town once drank bubbly out of her shoes or
        whether
    She was a governess with a good name
        In Church circles, if her
    Husband spoiled her or if she lost her son,
        Is by this time all one.
She survived whatever happened; she forgave;
        she became.

So the painter may please himself; give her an English park,
    Rice-fields in China, or a slum tenement;
        Make the sky light or dark;
    Put green plush behind her or a red brick wall.
        She will compose them all,
Centring the eye on their essential human element.

ATLANTIS

Being set on the idea
    Of getting to Atlantis,
You have discovered of course
    Only the Ship of Fools is
Making the voyage this year,
As gales of abnormal force
    Are predicted, and that you
    Must therefore, be ready to

Behave absurdly enough
    To pass for one of The Boys,
At least appearing to love
    Hard liquor, horseplay and noise.

Should storms, as may well happen,
    Drive you to anchor a week
In some old harbour-city
    Of Ionia, then speak
With her witty scholars, men
Who have proved there cannot be
    Such a place as Atlantis:
    Learn their logic, but notice
    How its subtlety betrays
        Their enormous simple grief;
    Thus they shall teach you the ways
    To doubt that you may believe.

If, later, you run aground
    Among the headlands of Thrace,
Where with torches all night long
    A naked barbaric race
Leaps frenziedly to the sound
Of conch and dissonant gong;
    On that stony savage shore
    Strip off your clothes and dance, for
Unless you are capable
    Of forgetting completely
About Atlantis, you will
    Never finish your journe

Again, should you come .o gay
    Carthage or Corint'., take part
In their endless ga¹-ty;
    And if in some bar a tart,
As she strokes your hair, should say
'This is Atlantis, dearie,'
    Listen with attentiveness

To her life-story: unless
You become acquainted now
   With each refuge that tries to
Counterfeit Atlantis, how
   Will you recognise the true?

Assuming you beach at last
   Near Atlantis, and begin
The terrible trek inland
   Through squalid woods and frozen
Tundras where all are soon lost;
If, forsaken then, you stand,
   Dismissal everywhere,
   Stone and snow, silence and air,
O remember the great dead
   And honour the fate you are,
Travelling and tormented,
   Dialectic and bizarre.

Stagger onward rejoicing;
   And even then if, perhaps
Having actually got
   To the last col, you collapse
With all Atlantis shining
Below you yet you cannot
   Descend, you should still be proud
Just to peep at Atlantis
   In a poetic vision:
Give thanks and lie down in peace,
   Having seen your salvation.

All the little household gods
   Have started crying, but say
Good-bye now, and put to sea.
   Farewell, dear friend, farewell: may
Hermes, master of the roads
And the four dwarf Kabiri,
   Protect and serve you always;

And may the Ancient of Days
Provide for all you must do
   His invisible guidance,
Lifting up, friend, upon you
   The light of His countenance.

DOOMSDAY SONG

Jumbled in one common box
Of their dark stupidity,
Orchid, swan, and Caesar lie;
Time that tires of everyone
Has corroded all the locks
Thrown away the key for fun.

In its cleft a torrent mocks
Prophets who in days gone by
Made a profit on each cry,
Persona grata now with none;
And a jackass language shocks
Poets who can only pun.

Silence settles on the clocks;
Nursing mothers point a sly
Index finger at a sky,
Crimson with the setting sun;
In the valley of the fox
Gleams the barrel of a gun.

Once we could have made the docks,
Now it is too late to fly;

Once too often you and I
Did what we should not have done;
Round the rampant rugged rocks
Rude and ragged rascals run.

SONG OF THE OLD SOLDIER

When the Sex War ended with the slaughter of the
    Grandmothers,
They found a bachelor's baby suffocating under them;
Somebody called him George and that was the end of it;
    They hitched him up to the Army.
    George, you old debutante,
    How did you get in the Army?

In the Retreat from Reason he deserted on his rocking-horse
And lived on a fairy's kindness till he tired of kicking her;
He smashed her spectacles and stole her check-book and
    mackintosh
    Then cruised his way back to the Army.
    George, you old numero,
    How did you get in the Army?

Before the Diet of Sugar he was using razor-blades
And exited soon after with an allergy to maidenheads;
He discovered a cure of his own, but no one would patent it,
    So he showed up again in the Army.
    George, you old flybynight,
    How did you get in the Army?

When the Vice Crusades were over he was hired by some
    Muscovites

Prospecting for deodorants among the Eskimos;
He was caught by a common cold and condemned to the
    whiskey mines,
  But schemozzled back to the Army.
  George, you old Emperor,
  How did you get in the Army?

Since Peace was signed with Honour he's been minding his
    business;
But, whoops, here comes His Idleness, buttoning his uniform;
Just in tidy time to massacre the Innocents;
  He's come home to roost in the Army.
  George, you old matador,
  Welcome back to the Army.

MUNDUS ET INFANS

FOR ARTHUR AND ANGELYN STEVENS

Kicking his mother until she let go of his soul
Has given him a healthy appetite: clearly, her role
  In the New Order must be
To supply and deliver his raw materials free;
  Should there be any shortage,
She will be held responsible; she also promises
To show him all such attentions as befit his age.
  Having dictated peace,

With one fist clenched behind his head, heel drawn up to thigh,
The cocky little ogre dozes off, ready,
  Though, to take on the rest

Of the world at the drop of a hat or the mildest
  Nudge of the impossible,
Resolved, cost what it may, to seize supreme power and
Sworn to resist tyranny to the death with all
  Forces at his command.

A pantheist not a solipsist, he co-operates
With a universe of large and noisy feeling-states
  Without troubling to place
Them anywhere special, for, to his eyes, Funnyface
  Or Elephant as yet
Mean nothing. His distinction between Me and Us
Is a matter of taste; his seasons are Dry and Wet;
  He thinks as his mouth does.

Still his loud iniquity is still what only the
Greatest of saints become—someone who does not lie:
  He because he cannot
Stop the vivid present to think, they by having got
  Past reflection into
A passionate obedience in time. We have our Boy-
Meets-Girl era of mirrors and muddle to work through,
  Without rest, without joy.

Therefore we love him because his judgments are so
Frankly subjective that his abuse carries no
  Personal sting. We should
Never dare offer our helplessness as a good
  Bargain, without at least
Promising to overcome a misfortune we blame
History or Banks or the Weather for; but this beast
  Dares to exist without shame.

Let him praise our Creator with the top of his voice,
Then, and the motions of his bowels; let us rejoice
  That he lets us hope, for
He may never become a fashionable or
  Important personage;

However bad he may be, he has not yet gone mad;
Whoever we are now, we were no worse at his age:
    So of course we ought to be glad

When he bawls the house down. Has he not a perfect right
To remind us at every moment how we quite
    Rightly expect each other
To go upstairs or for a walk if we must cry over
    Spilt milk, such as our wish
That, since, apparently, we shall never be above
Either or both, we had never learned to distinguish
    Between hunger and love?

THE LESSON

The first time that I dreamed, we were in flight,
And fagged with running; there was civil war,
A valley full of thieves and wounded bears.

Farms blazed behind us; turning to the right,
We came at once to a tall house, its door
Wide open, waiting for its long-lost heirs.

An elderly clerk sat on the bedroom stairs
Writing; but we had tiptoed past him when
He raised his head and stuttered—'Go away.'
We wept and begged to stay:
He wiped his pince-nez, hesitated, then
Said no, he had no power to give us leave;
Our lives were not in order; we must leave.

*   *   *

The second dream began in a May wood;
We had been laughing; your blue eyes were kind,
Your excellent nakedness without disdain.

Our lips met, wishing universal good;
But on their impact sudden flame and wind
Fetched you away and turned me loose again

To make a focus for a wide wild plain,
Dead level and dead silent and bone dry,
Where nothing could have suffered, sinned, or grown.
On a high chair alone
I sat, my little master, asking why
The cold and solid object in my hands
Should be a human hand, one of your hands.

* * *

And the last dream was this: we were to go
To a great banquet and a Victory Ball
After some tournament or dangerous test.

Only our seats had velvet cushions, so
We must have won; though there were crowns for all,
Ours were of gold, of paper all the rest.

O fair or funny was each famous guest.
Love smiled at Courage over priceless glass,
And rockets died in hundreds to express
Our learned carelessness.
A band struck up; all over the green grass
A sea of paper crowns rose up to dance:
Ours were too heavy; we did not dance.

* * *

I woke. You were not there. But as I dressed
Anxiety turned to shame, feeling all three
Intended one rebuke. For had not each

In its own way tried to teach
My will to love you that it cannot be,
As I think, of such consequence to want
What anyone is given, if they want?

INVOCATION TO ARIEL

Sing, Ariel, sing,
Sweetly, dangerously
Out of the sour
And shiftless water,
Lucidly out
Of the dozing tree,
Entrancing, rebuking
The raging heart
With a smoother song
Than this rough world,
Unfeeling god.

O brilliantly, lightly,
Of separation,
Of bodies and death,
Unanxious one, sing
To man, meaning me,
As now, meaning always,
In love or out,
Whatever that mean,
Trembling he takes
The silent passage
Into discomfort.

STEPHANO'S SONG

Embrace me, belly, like a bride;
Dear daughter, for the weight you drew
From humble pie and swallowed pride,
Believe the boast in which you grew;
Where mind meets matter, both should woo;
Together let us learn that game
The high play better than the blue:
A lost thing looks for a lost name.

Behind your skirts your son must hide
When disappointments bark and boo;
Brush my heroic ghosts aside,
Wise nanny, with a vulgar pooh;
Exchanging cravings we pursue
Alternately a single aim:
Between the bottle and the 'loo'
A lost thing looks for a lost name.

Though in the long run satisfied,
The will of one by being two
At every moment is denied;
Exhausted glasses wonder who
Is self and sovereign, I or You?
We cannot both be what we claim,
The real Stephano—Which is true?
A lost thing looks for a lost name.

Child? Mother? Either grief will do;
The need for pardon is the same,
The contradiction is not new:
A lost thing looks for a lost name.

TRINCULO'S SONG

Mechanic, merchant, king,
Are warmed by the cold clown
Whose head is in the clouds
And never can get down.

Into a solitude
Undreamed of by their fat
Quick dreams have lifted me;
The north wind steals my hat.

On clear days I can see
Green acres far below,
And the red roof where I
Was Little Trinculo.

There lies that solid world
These hands can never reach;
My history, my love,
Is but a choice of speech.

A terror shakes my tree,
A flock of words fly out,
Whereat a laughter shakes
The busy and devout.

Wild images, come down
Out of your freezing sky,
That I, like shorter men,
May get my joke and die.

ALONSO TO FERDINAND

Dear Son, when the warm multitudes cry,
Ascend your throne majestically,
But keep in mind the waters where fish
See sceptres descending with no wish
To touch them; sit regal and erect,
But imagine the sands where a crown
Has the status of a broken-down
Sofa or mutilated statue:
Remember as bells and cannon boom
The cold deep that does not envy you,
The sunburnt superficial kingdom
Where a king is an object.

Expect no help from others, for who
Talk sense to princes or refer to
The scorpion in official speeches
As they unveil some granite Progress
Leading a child and holding a bunch
Of lilies? In their Royal Zoos the
Shark and the octopus are tactfully
Omitted; synchronized clocks march on
Within their powers; without, remain
The ocean flats where no subscription
Concerts are given, the desert plain
Where there is nothing for lunch.

Only your darkness can tell you what
A prince's ornate mirror dare not,
Which you should fear more—the sea in which
A tyrant sinks entangled in rich
Robes while a mistress turns a white back
Upon his splutter, or the desert
Where an emperor stands in his shirt
While his diary is read by sneering
Beggars, and far off he notices
A lean horror flapping and hopping

Toward him with inhuman swiftness:
Learn from your dreams what you lack,

For as your fears are, so must you hope.
The Way of Justice is a tightrope
Where no prince is safe for one instant
Unless he trust his embarrassment,
As in his left ear the siren sings
Meltingly of water and a night
Where all flesh had peace, and on his right
The efreet offers a brilliant void
Where his mind could be perfectly clear
And all his limitations destroyed:
Many young princes soon disappear
To join all the unjust kings.

So, if you prosper, suspect those bright
Mornings when you whistle with a light
Heart. You are loved; you have never seen
The harbour so still, the park so green,
So many well-fed pigeons upon
Cupolas and triumphal arches,
So many stags and slender ladies
Beside the canals. Remember when
Your climate seems a permanent home
For marvellous creatures and great men,
What griefs and convulsions startled Rome,
Ecbatana, Babylon.

How narrow the space, how slight the chance
For civil pattern and importance
Between the watery vagueness and
The triviality of the sand,
How soon the lively trip is over
From loose craving to sharp aversion,
Aimless jelly to paralyzed bone;
At the end of each successful day
Remember that the fire and the ice

Are never more than one step away
From the temperate city: it is
But a moment to either.

But should you fail to keep your kingdom
And, like your father before you, come
Where thought accuses and feeling mocks,
Believe your pain; praise the scorching rocks
For their desiccation of your lust,
Thank the bitter treatment of the tide
For its dissolution of your pride,
That the whirlwind may arrange your will
And the deluge release it to find
The spring in the desert, the fruitful
Island in the sea, where flesh and mind
Are delivered from mistrust.

Blue the sky beyond her humming sail
As I sit today by our ship's rail
Watching exuberant porpoises
Escort us homeward and writing this
For you to open when I am gone:
Read it, Ferdinand, with the blessing
Of Alonso, your father, once King
Of Naples, now ready to welcome
Death, but rejoicing in a new love,
A new peace, having heard the solemn
Music strike and seen the statue move
To forgive our illusion.

SONG OF THE MASTER AND BOATSWAIN

At Dirty Dick's and Sloppy Joe's
    We drank our liquor straight,
Some went upstairs with Margery,
    And some, alas, with Kate;
And two by two like cat and mouse
The homeless played at keeping house.

There Wealthy Meg, the Sailor's Friend,
    And Marion, cow-eyed,
Opened their arms to me but I
    Refused to step inside;
I was not looking for a cage
In which to mope in my old age.

The nightingales are sobbing in
    The orchards of our mothers,
And hearts that we broke long ago
    Have long been breaking others;
Tears are round, the sea is deep:
Roll them overboard and sleep.

MIRANDA'S SONG — *vilanelle*

My Dear One is mine as mirrors are lonely,
As the poor and sad are real to the good king,
And the high green hill sits always by the sea.

Up jumped the Black Man behind the elder tree,
Turned a somersault and ran away waving;
My Dear One is mine as mirrors are lonely.

The Witch gave a squawk; her venomous body
Melted into light as water leaves a spring
And the high green hill sits always by the sea.

At his crossroads, too, the Ancient prayed for me;
Down his wasted cheeks tears of joy were running:
My Dear One is mine as mirrors are lonely.

He kissed me awake, and no one was sorry;
The sun shone on sails, eyes, pebbles, anything,
And the high green hill sits always by the sea.

So, to remember our changing garden, we
Are linked as children in a circle dancing:
My Dear One is mine as mirrors are lonely,
And the high green hill sits always by the sea.

CALIBAN TO THE AUDIENCE

If now, having dismissed your hired impersonators with ver-
dicts ranging from the laudatory orchid to the disgusted and
disgusting egg, you ask and, of course, notwithstanding the
conscious fact of his irrevocable absence, you instinctively *do*
ask for our so good, so great, so dead author to stand before
the finally lowered curtain and take his shyly responsible bow
for this, his latest, ripest production, it is I—my reluctance is,
I can assure you, co-equal with your dismay—who will always
loom thus wretchedly into your confused picture, for, in default
of the all-wise, all explaining master you would speak *to,* who
else at least can, who else indeed must respond to your bewil-

dered cry, but its very echo, the begged question you would speak to him *about*.

* * *

We must own [*for the present I speak your echo*] to a nervous perplexity not unmixed, frankly, with downright resentment. How *can* we grant the indulgence for which in his epilogue your personified type of the creative so lamely, tamely pleaded? Imprisoned, by you, in the mood doubtful, loaded, by you, with distressing embarrassments, we are, we submit, in no position to set *anyone* free.

Our native Muse, heaven knows and heaven be praised, is not exclusive. Whether out of the innocence of a child-like heart to whom all things are pure, or with the serenity of a status so majestic that the mere keeping up of tones and appearances, the suburban wonder as to what the strait-laced Unities might possibly think, or sad sour Probability possibly say, are questions for which she doesn't because she needn't, she hasn't in her lofty maturity any longer, to care a rap, she invites, dear generous-hearted creature that she is, just *tout le monde* to drop in at any time so that her famous, memorable, sought-after evenings present to the speculative eye an ever-shining, never-tarnished proof of her amazing unheard-of power to combine and happily contrast, to make *every* shade of the social and moral palette contribute to the general richness, of the skill, unapproached and unattempted by Grecian aunt or Gallic sister, with which she can skate full tilt toward the forbidden incoherence and then, in the last split second, on the shuddering edge of the bohemian standardless abyss, effect her breathtaking triumphant turn.

No timid segregation by rank or taste for her, no prudent listing into those who will, who might, who certainly would not, get on, no nicely graded scale of invitations to heroic formal Tuesdays, young comic Thursdays, al fresco farcical Saturdays. No, the real, the only, test of the theatrical as of the gastronomic, her practice confidently wagers, is the mixed perfected brew.

As he looks in on her, so marvellously at home with all her

cosy swarm about her, what accents will not assault the new arrival's ear, the magnificent tropes of tragic defiance and despair, the repartee of the high humour, the pun of the very low, cultured drawl and manly illiterate bellow, yet all of them gratefully doing their huge or tiny best to make the party go?

And if, assured by her smiling wave that of course he may, he should presently set out to explore her vast and rambling mansion, to do honour to its dear odd geniuses of local convenience and proportion, its multiplied deities of mysterious stair and interesting alcove, not one of the laughing groups and engrossed warmed couples that he keeps 'surprising'—the never-ending surprise for him is that he doesn't seem to—but affords some sharper instance of relations he would have been the last to guess at, choleric prince at his ease with lymphatic butler, moist handtaking so to dry, youth getting on quite famously with stingy cold old age, some stranger vision of the large loud liberty violently rocking yet never, he is persuaded, finally upsetting the jolly crowded boat.

What, he may well ask, has the gracious goddess done to all these people that, at her most casual hint, they should so trustingly, so immediately take off those heavy habits one thinks of them as having for their health and happiness day and night to wear, without in this unfamiliar unbuttoned state —the notable absence of the slightest shiver or not-quite-inhibited sneeze is indication positive—for a second feeling the draught? Is there, could there be, *any* miraculous suspension of the wearily historic, the dingily geographic, the dully drearily sensible beyond her faith, her charm, her love, to command? Yes, there could be, yes, alas, indeed yes, O there is, right here, right now before us, the situation present.

How *could* you, you who are one of the oldest habitués at these delightful functions, one, possibly the closest, of her trusted inner circle, how could you be guilty of the incredible unpardonable treachery of bringing along the one creature, as you above all men must have known, whom she cannot and will not under any circumstances stand, the solitary exception she is not at any hour of the day or night at home to, the unique case that her attendant spirits have absolute instructions never, neither at the front door nor at the back, to admit?

At Him and at Him only does she draw the line, not because there are any limits to her sympathy but precisely because there are none. Just because of all she is and all she means to be, she cannot conceivably tolerate in her presence the represented principle of *not* sympathizing, *not* associating, *not* amusing, the only child of her Awful Enemy, the rival whose real name she will never sully her lips with—'that envious witch' is sign sufficient—who does not rule but defiantly is the unrectored chaos.

All along and only too well she has known what would happen if, by any careless mischance—of conscious malice she never dreamed till now—He should ever manage to get in. She foresaw what He would do to the conversation, lying in wait for its vision of private love or public justice to warm to an Egyptian brilliance and then with some fish-like odour or *bruit insolite* snatching the visionaries back tongue-tied and blushing to the here and now; she foresaw what He would do to the arrangements, breaking, by a refusal to keep in step, the excellent order of the dancing ring, and ruining supper by knocking over the loaded appetizing tray; worst of all, she foresaw, she dreaded, what He would end up by doing to her, that, not content with upsetting her guests, with spoiling their fun, His progress from outrage to outrage would not relent before the gross climax of His making, horror unspeakable, a pass at her virgin self.

Let us suppose, even, that in your eyes she is by no means as we have always fondly imagined, your dear friend, that what we have just witnessed was not what it seemed to us, the inexplicable betrayal of a life-long sacred loyalty, but your long-premeditated just revenge, the final evening up of some ancient never-forgotten score, then even so, why make us suffer who have never, in all conscience, done you harm? Surely the theatrical relation, no less than the marital, is governed by the sanely decent general law that, before visitors, in front of the children or the servants, there shall be no indiscreet revelation of animosity, no 'scenes', that, no matter to what intolerable degrees of internal temperature and pressure restraint may raise both the injured and the guilty, nevertheless such restraint is applied to tones and topics, the exhibited picture must be still as always the calm and smiling one the most malicious observer can see nothing wrong with, and not until the last of those whom manifested anger or mistrust would embarrass or amuse or not be good for have gone away or out or up, is the voice raised, the table thumped, the suspicious letter snatched at or the outrageous bill furiously waved.

For we, after all—you cannot have forgotten this—are strangers to her. We have never claimed her acquaintance, knowing as well as she that we do not and never could belong on her side of the curtain. All we have ever asked for is that for a few hours the curtain should be left undrawn, so as to allow our humble ragged selves the privilege of craning and gaping at the splendid goings-on inside. We most emphatically do *not* ask that she should speak to us, or try to understand us; on the contrary our one desire has always been that she should preserve for ever her old high strangeness, for what delights us about her world is just that it neither is nor possibly could become one in which we could breathe or behave, that in her house the right of innocent passage should remain so universal that the same neutral space accommodates the conspirator and his victim; the generals of both armies, the chorus of patriots and the choir of nuns, palace and farmyard, cathedral and smugglers' cave, that time should never revert to that intransigent element we are so ineluctably and only too familiarly in, but remain the passive good-natured creature she and her friends can by common consent do anything they like with —(it is not surprising that they should take advantage of their strange power and so frequently skip hours and days and even years: the dramatic mystery is that they should always so unanimously agree upon exactly how many hours and days and years to skip)—that upon their special constitutions the moral law should continue to operate so exactly that the timid not only deserve but actually win the fair, and it is the socially and physically unemphatic David who lays low the gorilla-chested Goliath with one well-aimed custard pie, that in their blessed climate, the manifestation of the inner life should always remain so easy and habitual that a sudden eruption of musical and metaphorical power is instantly recognized as standing for grief and disgust, an elegant *contrapposto* for violent death, and that consequently the picture which they in there present to us out here is always that of the perfectly tidiable case of disorder, the beautiful and serious problem exquisitely set without a single superfluous datum and insoluble with less, the expert landing of all the passengers with all their luggage safe and sound in the best of health and spirits and without so much as a scratch or a bruise.

Into that world of freedom without anxiety, sincerity without loss of vigour, feeling that loosens rather than ties the tongue, we are not, we reiterate, so blinded by presumption to our proper status and interest as to expect or even wish at any time to enter, far less to dwell there.

Must we—it seems oddly that we must—remind you that our existence does not, like hers, enjoy an infinitely indicative mood, an eternally present tense, a limitlessly active voice, for in our shambling, slovenly makeshift world any two persons, whether domestic first or neighbourly second, require and necessarily presuppose, in both their numbers and in all their cases, the whole inflected gamut of an alien third, since, without a despised or dreaded Them to turn the back *on,* there could be no intimate or affectionate Us to turn the eye *to;* that, *chez nous,* space is never the whole uninhabited circle but always some segment, its eminent domain upheld by two co-ordinates. There always has been and always will be, not only the vertical boundary, the river on this side of which initiative and honesty stroll arm in arm wearing sensible clothes, and beyond which is a savage elsewhere swarming with contagious diseases, but also its horizontal counterpart, the railroad above which houses stand in their own grounds, each equipped with a garage and a beautiful woman, sometimes with several, and below which huddled shacks provide a squeezing shelter to collarless herds who eat blancmange and have never said anything witty. Make the case as special as you please; take the tamest congregation or the wildest faction; take, say, a college. What river and railroad did for the grosser instance, lawn and corridor do for the more refined, dividing the tender who value from the tough who measure, the superstitious who still sacrifice to causation from the heretics who have already reduced the worship of truth to bare description, and so creating the academic fields to be guarded with umbrella and learned periodical against the trespass of any unqualified stranger not a whit less jealously than the game-preserve is protected from the poacher by the unamiable shot-gun. For without these prohibitive frontiers we should never know who we were or what we wanted. It is they who donate to neighbourhood all its accuracy and vehemence. It is thanks to them that we do know with whom to associate, make love, exchange recipes and jokes, go mountain climbing or sit side by side fishing from piers. It is thanks to them, too, that we know against whom to rebel. We *can* shock our parents by visiting the dives below the railroad tracks, we *can* amuse ourselves on what would otherwise have been a very dull evening indeed, in plotting to seize the post office across the river.

Of course these several private regions must together comprise one public whole—we would never deny that logic and instinct require that—of course We and They are united in the candid glare of the same commercial hope by day, and the soft refulgence of the same erotic nostalgia by night—and this is our point—without our privacies of situation, our local idioms of triumph and mishap, our different doctrines concerning the transubstantiation of the larger pinker bun on the terrestrial dish for which the mature sense may reasonably water and the adult fingers furtively or unabashedly go for, our specific choices of which hill it would be romantic to fly away over or what sea it would be exciting to run away to, our peculiar visions of the absolute stranger with a spontaneous longing for the lost who will adopt our misery not out of desire but pure compassion, without, in short, our devoted pungent expression of the partial and contrasted, the Whole would have no importance and its Day and Night no interest.

So, too, with Time who, in our auditorium, is not her dear old buffer so anxious to please everybody, but a prim magistrate whose court never adjourns, and from whose decisions, as he laconically sentences one to loss of hair and talent, another to seven days' chastity, and a third to boredom for life, there is no appeal. We should not be sitting here now, washed, warm, well-fed, in seats we have paid for, unless there were others who are not here; our liveliness and good-humour, such as they are, are those of survivors, conscious that there are others who have not been so fortunate, others who did not succeed in navigating the narrow passage or to whom the natives were not friendly, others whose streets were chosen by the explosion or through whose country the famine turned aside from ours to go, others who failed to repel the invasion of bacteria or to crush the insurrection of their bowels, others who lost their suit against their parents or were ruined by wishes they could not adjust or murdered by resentments they could not control; aware of some who were better and bigger but from whom, only the other day, Fortune withdrew her hand in sudden disgust, now nervously playing chess with drunken sea-captains in sordid cafés on the equator or the Arctic Circle, or lying, only a few blocks away, strapped and screaming on iron beds or dropping to naked pieces in damp graves. And shouldn't you too, dear master, reflect—forgive us for mentioning it—that we might very well not have been attending a production of yours this evening, had not some other and, maybe—who can tell?—brighter, talent married a barmaid or turned religious and shy or gone down in a liner with all his manuscripts, the loss recorded only in the corner of some country newspaper below A Poultry Lover's Jottings?

You yourself, we seem to remember, have spoken of the conjured spectacle as 'a mirror held up to nature', a phrase misleading in its aphoristic sweep but indicative at least of one aspect of the relation between the real and the imagined, their mutual reversal of value, for isn't the essential artistic strangeness to which your citation of the sinisterly biased image would point just this: that on the far side of the mirror the general will to compose, to form at all costs a felicitous pattern, becomes the *necessary cause* of any particular effort to live or act or love or triumph or vary, instead of being as, in so far as it emerges at all, it is on this side, their *accidental effect?*

Does Ariel—to nominate the spirit of reflection in your terms—call for manifestation? Then neither modesty nor fear of reprisals excuses the one so called on from publicly confessing that she cheated at croquet or that he committed incest in a dream. Does He demand concealment? Then their nearest and dearest must be deceived by disguises of sex and age which anywhere else would at once attract the attentions of the police or the derisive whistle of the awful schoolboy. That is the price asked, and how promptly and gladly paid, for universal reconciliation and peace, for the privilege of all galloping together past the finishing post neck and neck.

How then, we continue to wonder, knowing all this, could you act as if you did not, as if you did not realize that the embarrassing compresence of the absolutely natural, incorrigibly right-handed, and, to any request for co-operation, utterly negative, with the enthusiastically self-effacing would be a simultaneous violation of both worlds, as if you were not perfectly well aware that the magical musical condition, the orphic spell that turns the fierce dumb greedy beasts into grateful guides and oracles who will gladly take one anywhere and tell one everything free of charge, is precisely and simply that of his finite immediate note *not,* under any circumstances, being struck, of its not being tentatively whispered, far less positively banged.

Are we not bound to conclude, then, that, whatever snub to the poetic you may have intended incidentally to administer, your profounder motive in so introducing Him to them among whom, because He doesn't belong, He couldn't appear as anything but His distorted parody, a deformed and savage slave, was to deal a mortal face-slapping insult to us among whom He does and is, moreover, all grossness turned to glory, no less a person than the nude august elated archer of our heaven, the darling single son of Her who, in her right milieu, is certainly no witch but the most sensible of all the gods, whose influence is as sound as it is pandemic, on the race-track no less than in the sleeping cars of the Orient Express, our great white Queen of Love herself?

But even that is not the worst we suspect you of. If your words have not buttered any parsnips, neither have they broken any bones.

He, after all, can come back to us now to be comforted and respected, perhaps, after the experience of finding himself for a few hours and for the first time in His life not wanted, more fully and freshly appreciative of our affection than He has always been in the past: as for His dear mother, She is far too grand and far too busy to hear or care what you say or think. If only we were certain that your malice was confined to the verbal affront, we should long ago have demanded our money back and gone whistling home to bed. Alas, in addition to resenting what you have openly said, we fear even more what you may secretly have done. Is it possible that, not content with inveigling Caliban into Ariel's kingdom, you have also let loose Ariel in Caliban's? We note with alarm that when the other members of the final tableau were dismissed, He was not returned to His arboreal confinement as He should have been. Where is He now? For if the intrusion of the real has disconcerted and incommoded the poetic, that is a mere bagatelle compared to the damage which the poetic would inflict if it ever succeeded in intruding upon the real. We want no Ariel here, breaking down our picket fences in the name of fraternity, seducing our wives in the name of romance, and robbing us of our sacred pecuniary deposits in the name of justice. Where is Ariel? What have you done with Him? For we won't, we daren't, leave until you give us a satisfactory answer.

* * *

Such (*let me cease to play your echo and return to my officially natural role*)—such are your questions, are they not, but before I try to deal with them, I must ask for your patience, while I deliver a special message for our late author to those few among you, if indeed there be any—I have certainly heard no comment yet from them—who have come here, not to be entertained but to learn; that is, to any gay apprentice in the magical art who may have chosen this specimen of the prestidigitory genus to study this evening in the hope of grasping more clearly just how the artistic contraption works, of observing some fresh detail in the complex process by which the heady wine of amusement is distilled from the grape of composition. The rest of you I must beg for a little while to sit back and relax as the remarks I have now to make do not concern you; your turn will follow later.

* * *

So, strange young man—it is at his command, remember, that I say this to you; whether I agree with it or not is neither here nor there—you have decided on the conjurer's profession. Somewhere, in the middle of a salt marsh or at the bottom of a kitchen garden or on the top of a bus, you heard imprisoned Ariel call for help, and it is now a liberator's face that congratulates you from your shaving mirror every morning. As you walk the cold streets hatless, or sit over coffee and doughnuts in the corner of a cheap restaurant, your secret has already set you apart from the howling merchants and transacting multitudes to watch with fascinated distaste the bellowing barging banging passage of the awkward profit-seeking elbow, the dazed eye of the gregarious acquisitive condition. Lying awake at night in your single bed you are conscious of a power by which you will survive the wallpaper of your boarding-house or the expensive bourgeois horrors of your home. Yes, Ariel is grateful; He does come when you call, He does tell you all the gossip He overhears on the stairs, all the goings-on He observes through the keyhole; he really is willing to arrange anything you care to ask for, and you are rapidly finding out the right orders to give—who should be killed in the hunting accident, which couple to send into the cast-iron shelter, what scent will arouse a Norwegian engineer, how to get the young hero from the country lawyer's office to the Princess's reception, when to mislay the letter, where the cabinet minister should be reminded of his mother, why the dishonest valet must be a martyr to indigestion but immune from the common cold.

As the gay productive months slip by, in spite of fretful discouraged days, of awkward moments of misunderstanding or rather, seen retrospectively as happily cleared up and got over, verily because of them, you are definitely getting the hang of this, at first so novel and bewildering, relationship between magician and familiar, whose duty it is to sustain your infinite conceptual appetite with vivid concrete experiences. And, as the months turn into years, your wonder-working romance into an economical habit, the encountered case of good or evil in our wide world of property and boredom which leaves you confessedly and unsympathetically at a loss, the aberrant phase in the whole human cycle of ecstasy and exhaustion with which you are imperfectly familiar, become increasingly rare. No perception however *petite,* no notion however subtle, escapes your attention or baffles your understanding: on entering any room you immediately distinguish the wasters who throw away their fruit half-eaten from the preservers who bottle all the summer; as the passengers file down the ship's gangway you unerringly guess which suitcase contains indecent novels; a five-minute chat about the weather or the coming elections is all you require to diagnose any distemper, however self-assured, for by then your eye has already spotted the tremor of the lips in that infinitesimal moment while the lie was getting its balance, your ear already picked up the heart's low whimper which the capering legs were determined to stifle, your nose detected on love's breath the trace of *ennui* which foretells his early death, or the despair just starting to smoulder at the base of the scholar's brain which years hence will suddenly blow it up with one appalling laugh: in every case you can prescribe the saving treatment called for, knowing at once when it may be gentle and remedial when all that is needed is soft music and a pretty girl, and when it must be drastic and surgical, when nothing will do any good but political disgrace or financial and erotic failure. If I seem to attribute these powers to you when the eyes, the ears, the nose, the putting two and two together are, of course, all His, and yours only the primitive wish to know, it is a rhetorical habit I have caught from your, in the main juvenile and feminine, admirers whose naive unawareness of whom they ought properly to thank and praise you see no point in, for mere accuracy's stuffy sake, correcting.

Anyway, the partnership is a brilliant success. On you go together to ever greater and faster triumphs; ever more major grows the accumulated work, ever more masterly the manner, sound even at its pale sententious worst, and at its best the rich red personal flower of the grave and grand, until one day which you can never either at the time or later identify exactly, your strange fever reaches its crisis and from now on begins, ever so slowly, maybe to subside. At first you cannot tell what or why is the matter; you have only a vague feeling that it is no longer between you so smooth and sweet as it used to be. Sour silences appear, at first only for an occasional moment, but progressively more frequently and more prolonged, curdled moods in which you cannot for the life of you think of any request to make, and His dumb standing around, waiting for orders gets inexplicably but maddeningly on your nerves, until presently, to your amazement, you hear yourself asking Him if He wouldn't like a vacation and are shocked by your feeling of intense disappointment when He who has always hitherto so immediately and recklessly taken your slightest hint, says gauchely 'No.' So it goes on from exasperated bad to desperate worst until you realize in despair that there is nothing for it but you two to part. Collecting all your strength for the distasteful task, you finally manage to stammer or shout 'You are free. Goodbye,' but to your dismay He whose obedience through all the enchanted years has never been less than perfect, now refuses to budge. Striding up to Him in fury, you glare into His unblinking eyes and stop dead, transfixed with horror at seeing reflected there, not what you had always expected to see, a conqueror smiling at a conqueror, both promising mountains and marvels, but a gibbering fist-clenched creature with which you are all too unfamiliar, for this is the first time indeed that you have met the only subject that you have, who is not a dream amenable to magic but the all too solid flesh you must acknowledge as your own; at last you have come face to face with me, and are appalled to learn how far I am from being, in any sense, your dish; how completely lacking in that poise and calm and all forgiving because all understanding good nature which to the

99

critical eye is so wonderfully and domestically present on every page of your published inventions.

But where, may I ask, should I have acquired them, when, like a society mother who, although she is, of course, as she tells everyone, absolutely *devoted* to her child, simply *cannot* leave the dinner table just now and really *must* be in Le Touquet tomorrow, and so leaves him in charge of servants she doesn't know or boarding schools she has never seen, you have never in all these years taken the faintest personal interest in me? 'Oh!' you protestingly gasp, 'but how can you say such a thing, after I've toiled and moiled and worked my fingers to the bone, trying to give you a good home, after all the hours I've spent planning wholesome nourishing meals for you, after all the things I've gone without so that you should have swimming lessons and piano lessons and a new bicycle. Have I ever let you go out in summer without your sun hat, or come in in winter without feeling your stockings and insisting, if they were the least bit damp, on your changing them at once? Haven't you always been allowed to do everything, in reason, that you liked?'

Exactly: even deliberate ill-treatment would have been less unkind. Gallows and battlefields are, after all, no less places of mutual concern than sofa and bridal-bed; the dashing flirtations of fighter pilots and the coy tactics of twirled moustache and fluttered fan, the gasping mud-caked wooing of the coarsest foes and the reverent rage of the highest-powered romance, the lover's nip and the grip of the torturer's tongs are all—ask Ariel—variants of one common type, the bracket within which life and death with such passionate gusto cohabit, to be distinguished solely by the plus or minus sign which stands before them, signs which He is able at any time and in either direction to switch, but the one exception, the sum no magic of His can ever transmute, is the indifferent zero. Had you tried to destroy me, had we wrestled through long dark hours, we might by daybreak have learnt something from each other; in some panting pause to recover breath for further more savage blows or in the moment before your death or mine, we might both have heard together that music which explains and pardons all.

Had you, on the other hand, really left me alone to go my whole free-wheeling way to disorder, to be drunk every day before lunch, to jump stark naked from bed to bed, to have a fit every week or a major operation every other year, to forge cheques or water the widow's stock, I might, after countless skids and punctures, have come by the bumpy third-class road of guilt and remorse smack into that very same truth which you were meanwhile admiring from your distant comfortable veranda but would never point out to me.

Such genuine escapades, though, might have disturbed the master at his meditations and even involved him in trouble with the police. The strains of oats, therefore, that you prudently permitted me to sow were each and all of an unmitigatedly minor wildness: a quick cold clasp now and then in some *louche* hotel to calm me down while you got on with the so thorough documentation of your great unhappy love for one who by being bad or dead or married provided you with the Good Right Subject that would never cease to bristle with importance; one bout of flu per winter, an occasional twinge of toothache, and enough tobacco to keep me in a good temper while you composed your melting eclogues of rustic piety; licence to break my shoelaces, spill soup on my tie, burn cigarette holes in the tablecloth, lose letters and borrowed books, and generally keep myself busy while you polished to a perfection your lyric praises of the more candid, more luxurious world to come.

Can you wonder then, when, as was bound to happen sooner or later, your charms, because they no longer amuse you, have cracked and your spirits, because you are tired of giving orders, have ceased to obey, and you are left alone with me, the dark thing you could never abide to be with, if I do not yield you kind answer or admire you for the achievements I was never allowed to profit from, if I resent hearing you speak of your neglect of me as your 'exile', of the pains you never took with me as 'all lost'?

But why continue? From now on we shall have, as we both know only too well, no company but each other's, and if I have had, as I consider, a good deal to put up with from you, I must own that, after all, I am not just the person I would have chosen for a life companion myself; so the only chance, which in any case is slim enough, of my getting a tolerably new master and you a tolerably new man, lies in our both learning, if possible and as soon as possible, to forgive and forget the past, and to keep our respective hopes for the future within moderate, very moderate, limits.

* * *

And now at last it is you, assorted, consorted specimens of the general popular type, the major flock who have trotted trustingly hither but found, you reproachfully baah, no grazing, that I turn to and address on behalf of Ariel and myself. To your questions I shall attempt no direct reply, for the mere fact that you have been able so anxiously to put them is in itself sufficient proof that you possess their answers. All your clamour signifies is this: that your first big crisis, the breaking of the childish spell in which, so long as it enclosed you, there was, for you, no mirror, no magic, for everything that happened was a miracle—it was just as extraordinary for a chair to be a chair as for it to turn into a horse; it was no more absurd that the girding on of coal-scuttle and poker should transform you into noble Hector than that you should have a father and mother who called you Tommy—and it was therefore only necessary for you to presuppose one genius, one unrivalled I to wish these wonders in all their endless plenitude and novelty to be, is, in relation to your present, behind, that your singular transparent globes of enchantment have shattered one by one, and you have now all come together in the larger colder emptier room on this side of the mirror which *does* force your eyes to recognize and reckon with the two of us, your ears to detect the irreconcilable difference between my reiterated affirmation of what your furnished circumstances categorically are, and His successive propositions as to everything else which they conditionally might be. You have, as I say, taken your first step.

The journey of life—the down-at-heels disillusioned figure can still put its characterization across—is infinitely long and its possible destinations infinitely distant from one another, but the time spent in actual travel is infinitesimally small. The hours the traveller measures are those in which he is at rest between the three or four decisive instants of transportation which are all he needs and all he gets to carry him the whole of his way; the scenery he observes is the view, gorgeous or drab, he glimpses from platform or siding; the incidents he thrills or blushes to remember take place in waiting and washrooms, ticket queues and parcels offices: it is in those promiscuous places of random association, in that air of anticipatory fidget, that he makes friends and enemies, that he promises, confesses, kisses, and betrays until, either because it is the one he has been expecting, or because, losing his temper, he has vowed to take the first to come along, or because he has been given a free ticket, or simply by misdirection or mistake, a train arrives which he does get into: it whistles—at least he thinks afterwards he remembers it whistling—but before he can blink, it has come to a standstill again and there he stands clutching his battered bags, surrounded by entirely strange smells and noises—yet in their smelliness and noisiness how familiar—one vast important stretch the nearer Nowhere, that still smashed terminus at which he will, in due course, be deposited, seedy and by himself.

Yes, you have made a definite start; you *have* left your homes way back in the farming provinces or way out in the suburban tundras, but whether you have been hanging around for years or have barely and breathlessly got here on one of those locals which keep arriving minute after minute, this is still only the main depot, the Grandly Average Place from which at odd hours the expresses leave seriously and sombrely for Somewhere, and where it is still possible for me to posit the suggestion that you go no farther. You will never, after all, feel better than in your present shaved and breakfasted state which there are restaurants and barber shops here indefinitely to preserve; you will never feel more secure than you do now in your knowledge that you *have* your ticket, your passport *is* in order, you have *not* forgotten to pack your pyjamas and an extra clean shirt; you will never have the same opportunity of learning about *all* the holy delectable spots of current or historic interest—an insistence on reaching *one* will necessarily exclude the others—than you have in these bepostered halls; you will never meet a jollier, more various crowd than you see around you here, sharing with you the throbbing, suppressed excitement of those to whom the exciting thing is still, perhaps, to happen. But once you leave, no matter in which direction, your next stop will be far outside this land of habit that so democratically stands up for your right to stagestruck hope, and well inside one of those, all equally foreign, uncomfortable and despotic, certainties of failure or success. Here at least I, and Ariel too, are free to warn you not, should we meet again there, to speak to either of us, not to engage either of us as your guide, but there we shall no longer be able to refuse you; then, unfortunately for you, we shall be compelled to say nothing and obey your fatal foolish commands. Here, whether you listen to me or not, and it's highly improbable that you will, I can at least warn you what will happen if at our next meeting you should insist—and that is all too probable, on putting one of us in charge.

'Release us,' you will beg, then, supposing it is I whom you make for—oh how awfully uniform, once one translates them out of your private lingoes of expression, all your sorrows are and how awfully well I know them—'release us from our minor roles. Carry me back, Master, to the cathedral town where the canons run through the water meadows with butterfly nets and the old women keep sweetshops in the cobbled side streets, or back to the upland mill town (gunpowder and plush) with its grope-movie and its pool-room lit by gas, carry me back to the days before my wife had put on weight, back to the years when beer was cheap and the rivers really froze in winter. Pity me, Captain, pity a poor old stranded sea-salt whom an unlucky voyage has wrecked on the desolate mahogany coast of this bar with nothing left him but his big moustache. Give me my passage home, let me see that harbour once again just as it was before I learned the bad words. Patriarchs wiser than Abraham mended their nets on the modest wharf; white and wonderful beings undressed on the sanddunes; sunset glittered on the plate-glass windows of the Marine Biological Station; far off on the extreme horizon a whale spouted. Look, Uncle, look. They have broken my glasses and I have lost my silver whistle. Pick me up, Uncle, let little Johnny ride away on your massive shoulders to recover his green kingdom, where the steam rollers are as friendly as the farm dogs and it would never become necessary to look over one's left shoulder or clench one's right fist in one's pocket. You cannot miss it. Black currant bushes hide the ruined opera house where badgers are said to breed in great numbers; an old horse-tramway winds away westward through suave foothills crowned with stone circles—follow it and by nightfall one would come to a large good-natured waterwheel—to the north, beyond a forest inhabited by charcoal burners, one can see the Devil's Bedposts quite distinctly, to the east the museum where for sixpence one can touch the ivory chessmen. O Cupid, Cupid, howls the whole dim chorus, take us home. We have never felt really well in this climate of distinct ideas; we have never been able to follow the regulations properly; Business, Science, Religion, Art, and all the other fictitious immortal persons who matter here have, frankly, not been very kind. We're so, so tired, the rewarding soup is stone cold, and over our blue wonders the grass grew long ago. O take us home with you, strong and swelling One, home to your promiscuous pastures where the minotaur of authority is just a roly-poly ruminant and nothing is at stake, those purring sites and amusing vistas where the fluctuating arabesques of sound, the continuous eruption of colours and scents, the whole rich incoherence of a nature made up of gaps and asymmetrical events plead beautifully and bravely for our undistress.'

And in that very moment when you so cry for deliverance from any and every anxious possibility, I shall have no option but to be faithful to my oath of service and instantly transport you, not indeed to any cathedral town or mill town or harbour or hillside or jungle or other specific Eden which your memory necessarily but falsely conceives of as the ultimately liberal condition, which in point of fact you have never known yet, but directly to that downright state itself. Here you are. This is it. Directly overhead a full moon casts a circle of dazzling light without any penumbra, exactly circumscribing its desolation in which every object is extraordinarily still and sharp. Cones of extinct volcanoes rise up abruptly from the lava plateau fissured by chasms and pitted with hot springs from which steam rises without interruption straight up into the windless rarefied atmosphere. Here and there a geyser erupts without warning, spouts furiously for a few seconds and as suddenly subsides. Here, where the possessive note is utterly silent and all events are tautological repetitions and no decision will ever alter the secular stagnation, at long last you are, as you have asked to be, the only subject. Who, When, Why, the poor tired little historic questions fall wilting into a hush of utter failure. Your tears splash down upon clinkers which will never be persuaded to recognize a neighbour and there is really and truly no one to appear with tea and help. You have indeed come all the way to the end of your bachelor's journey where Liberty stands with her hands behind her back, not caring, not minding *anything*. Confronted by a straight and snubbing stare to which mythology is bosh, surrounded by an infinite passivity and purely arithmetical disorder which is only open to perception, and with nowhere to go on to, your existence is indeed free at last to choose its own meaning, that is, to plunge headlong into despair and fall through silence fathomless and dry, all fact your single drop, all value your pure alas.

* * *

But what of that other, smaller but doubtless finer group among you, important persons at the top of the ladder, exhausted lions of the season, local authorities with their tense

106

tired faces, elderly hermits of both sexes living gloomily in the delta of a great fortune, whose *amour propre* prefers to turn for help to my more spiritual colleague.

'O yes,' you will sigh, 'we have had what once we would have called success. I moved the vices out of the city into a chain of reconditioned lighthouses. I introduced statistical methods into the Liberal Arts. I revived the country dances and installed electric stoves in the mountain cottages. I saved democracy by buying steel. I gave the caesura its freedom. But this world is no better and it is now quite clear to us that there is nothing to be done with such a ship of fools, adrift on a sugarloaf sea in which it is going very soon and suitably to founder. Deliver us, dear Spirit, from the tantrums of our telephones and the whispers of our secretaries conspiring against Man; deliver us from these helpless agglomerations of dishevelled creatures with their bed-wetting, vomiting, weeping bodies, their giggling, fugitive, disappointing hearts, and scrawling, blotted, misspelt minds, to whom we have so foolishly tried to bring the light they did not want; deliver us from all the litter of *billets-doux*, empty beer bottles, laundry lists, directives, promissory notes and broken toys, the terrible mess that this particularized life, which we have so futilely attempted to tidy, sullenly insists on leaving behind it; translate us, bright Angel, from this hell of inert and ailing matter, growing steadily senile in a time for ever immature, to that blessed realm, so far above the twelve impertinent winds and the four unreliable seasons, that Heaven of the Really General Case where, tortured no longer by three dimensions and immune from temporal vertigo, Life turns into Light, absorbed for good into the permanently stationary, completely self-sufficient, absolutely reasonable One.'

Obliged by the terms of His contract to gratify this other request of yours, the wish for freedom to transcend *any* condition, for direct unentailed power without *any*, however secretly immanent, obligation to inherit or transmit, what can poor shoulder-shrugging Ariel do but lead you forthwith into a nightmare which has all the wealth of exciting action and all the emotional poverty of an adventure story for boys, a state of perpetual emergency and everlasting improvisation where all is need and change.

All the phenomena of an empirically ordinary world are given. Extended objects appear to which events happen—old men catch dreadful coughs, little girls get their arms twisted, flames run whooping through woods, round a river bend, as harmless looking as a dirty old bearskin rug, comes the gliding fury of a town-effacing wave, but these are merely elements in an allegorical landscape to which mathematical measurement and phenomenological analysis have no relevance.

All the voluntary movements are possible—crawling through flues and old sewers, sauntering past shop-fronts, tiptoeing through quicksands and mined areas, running through derelict factories and across empty plains, jumping over brooks, diving into pools or swimming along between banks of roses, pulling at manholes or pushing at revolving doors, clinging to rotten balustrades, sucking at straws or wounds; all the modes of transport, letters, ox-carts, canoes, hansom cabs, trains, trolleys, cars, aeroplanes, balloons, are available, but any sense of direction, any knowledge of where on earth one has come from or where on earth one is going to is completely absent.

Religion and culture seem to be represented by a catholic belief that something is lacking which must be found, but as to what that something is, the keys of heaven, the missing heir, genius, the smells of childhood, or a sense of humour, why it is lacking, whether it has been deliberately stolen, or accidentally lost or just hidden for a lark, and who is responsible, our ancestors, ourselves, the social structure, or mysterious wicked powers, there are as many faiths as there are searchers, and clues can be found behind every clock, under every stone, and in every hollow tree to support all of them.

Again, other selves undoubtedly exist, but though everyone's pocket is bulging with birth certificates, insurance policies, passports and letters of credit, there is no way of proving whether they are genuine or planted or forged, so that no one knows whether another is his friend disguised as an enemy or his enemy disguised as a friend (there is probably no one whose real name is Brown), or whether the police, who here as elsewhere are grimly busy, are crushing a criminal revolt or upholding a vicious tyranny, any more than he knows whether he himself is a victim of the theft, or the thief, or a rival thief, a professionally interested detective or a professionally impartial journalist.

Even the circumstances of the tender passion, the long-distance calls, the assignation at the aquarium, the farewell embrace under the fish-tail burner on the landing, are continually present, but since, each time it goes through its performance, it never knows whether it is saving a life, or obtaining secret information, or forgetting or spiting its real love, the heart feels nothing but a dull percussion of conceptional foreboding. Everything, in short, suggests Mind but, surrounded by an infinite extension of the adolescent difficulty, a rising of the subjective and subjunctive to ever steeper, stormier heights, the panting frozen expressive gift has collapsed under the strain of its communicative anxiety, and contributes nothing by way of meaning but a series of staccato barks or a delirious gush of glossolalia.

And from this nightmare of public solitude, this everlasting Not Yet, what relief have you but in an ever giddier collective gallop, with bisson eye and bevel course, toward the gray horizon of the bleaker vision, what landmarks but the four dead rivers, the Joyless, the Flaming, the Mournful, and the Swamp of Tears, what goal but the black stone on which the bones are cracked, for only there in its cry of agony can your existence find at last an unequivocal meaning and your refusal to be yourself become a serious despair, the love nothing, the fear all?

* * *

Such are the alternative routes, the facile glad-handed highway or the virtuous averted track, by which the human effort to make its own fortune arrives all eager at its abruptly dreadful end. I have tried—the opportunity was not to be neglected —to raise the admonitory forefinger, to ring the alarming bell, but with so little confidence of producing the right result, so certain that the open eye and attentive ear will always interpret any sight and any sound to their advantage, every rebuff as a consolation, every prohibition as a rescue—that is what they open and attend for—that I find myself almost hoping, for your sake, that I have had the futile honour of addressing the blind and the deaf.

Having learnt his language, I begin to feel something of the serio-comic embarrassment of the dedicated dramatist, who, in representing to you your condition of estrangement from the truth, is doomed to fail the more he succeeds, for the more truthfully he paints the condition, the less clearly can he indicate the truth from which it is estranged, the brighter his revelation of the truth in its order, its justice, its joy, the fainter shows his picture of your actual condition in all its drabness and sham, and, worse still, the more sharply he defines the estrangement itself—and, ultimately, what other aim and justification has he, what else exactly *is* the artistic gift which he is forbidden to hide, if not to make you unforgettably conscious of the ungarnished offended gap between what you so questionably are and what you are commanded without any question to become, of the unqualified No that opposes your every step in any direction?—the more he must strengthen your delusion that an awareness of the gap is in itself a bridge, your interest in your imprisonment a release, so that, far from your being led by him to contrition and surrender, the regarding of your defects in his mirror, your dialogue, using his words, with yourself about yourself, becomes the one activity which never, like devouring or collecting or spending, lets you down, the one game which can be guaranteed, whatever the company, to catch on, a madness of which you can only be cured by some shock quite outside his control, an unpredictable misting over of his glass or an absurd misprint in his text.

Our unfortunate dramatist, therefore, is placed in the unseemly predicament of having to give all his passion, all his skill, all his time to the task of 'doing' life—consciously to give anything less than all would be a gross betrayal of his gift and an unpardonable presumption—as if it lay in *his* power to solve this dilemma—yet of having at the same time to hope that some unforeseen mishap will intervene to ruin his effect, without, however, obliterating your disappointment, the expectation aroused by him that there was an effect to ruin, that, if the smiling interest never did arrive, it must, through no fault of its own, have got stuck somewhere; that, exhausted, ravenous, delayed by fog, mobbed and mauled by a thousand irrelevancies, it has, nevertheless, not forgotten its promise but is still trying desperately to get a connection.

Beating about for some large loose image to define the original drama which aroused his imitative passion, the first performance in which the players were their own audience, the worldly stage on which their behaving flesh was really sore and sorry—for the floods of tears were not caused by onions, the deformities and wounds did not come off after a good wash, the self-stabbed heroine could not pick herself up again to make a gracious bow nor her seducer go demurely home to his plain and middle-aged spouse—the fancy immediately flushed is of the greatest grandest opera rendered by a very provincial touring company indeed.

Our performance—for Ariel and I are, you know this now, just as deeply involved as any of you—which we were obliged, all of us, to go on with and sit through right to the final dissonant chord, has been so indescribably inexcusably awful. Sweating and shivering in our moth-eaten ill-fitting stock costumes which with only a change of hat and re-arrangement of safety-pins, had to do for the *landsknecht* and the Parisian art-student, bumping into, now a rippling palace, now a primeval forest full of holes, at cross purposes with the scraping bleating orchestra we could scarcely hear for half the instruments were missing and the cottage piano which was filling-out must have stood for too many years in some damp parlour, we floundered on from fiasco to fiasco, the schmalz tenor never quite able at his big moments to get right up nor the ham bass right down, the stud contralto gargling through her maternal grief, the ravished coloratura trilling madly off-key and the reunited lovers half a bar apart, the knock-kneed armies shuffling limply through their bloody battles, the unearthly harvesters hysterically entangled in their honest fugato.

Now it is over. No, we have not dreamt it. Here we really stand, down stage with red faces and no applause; no effect, however simple, no piece of business, however unimportant, came off; there was not a single aspect of our whole production, not even the huge stuffed bird of happiness, for which a kind word could, however patronizingly, be said.

Yet, at this very moment when we do at last see ourselves as we are, neither cosy nor playful, but swaying out on the ultimate wind-whipped cornice that overhangs the unabiding void—we have never stood anywhere else—when our reasons are silenced by the heavy huge derision—There is nothing to say—there never has been—and our wills chuck in their hands —there is no way out—there never was—it is at this moment that for the first time in our lives we hear, not the sounds which, as born actors, we have hitherto condescended to use as an excellent vehicle for displaying our personalities and looks, but the real Word which is our only *raison d'être*. Not that we have improved; everything, the massacres, the whippings, the lies, the twaddle, and all their carbon copies are still present, more obviously than ever; nothing has been reconstructed; our shame, our fear, our incorrigible staginess, all wish and no resolve, are still, and more intensely than ever, all we have: only now it is not in spite of them but with them that we are blessed by that Wholly Other Life from which we are separated by an essential emphatic gulf of which our contrived fissures of mirror and proscenium arch—we understand them at last—are feebly figurative signs, so that all our meanings are reversed and it is precisely in its negative image of Judgment that we can positively envisage Mercy; it is just here, among the ruins and the bones, that we may rejoice in the perfected Work which is not ours. Its great coherences stand out through our secular blur in all their overwhelmingly righteous obligation; its voice speaks through our muffling banks of artificial flowers and unflinchingly delivers its authentic molar pardon; its spaces greet us with all their grand old prospect of wonder and width; the working charm is the full bloom of the unbothered state; the sounded note is the restored relation.

THREE DREAMS

I

How still it is; our horses
Have moved into the shade, our mothers
Have followed their migrating gardens.

Curlews on kettle moraines
Foretell the end of time,
The doom of paradox.

But lovelorn sighs ascend
From wretched greedy regions
Which cannot include themselves,

And a freckled orphan flinging
Ducks and drakes at a pond,
Stops looking for stones

And wishes he were a steamboat,
Or Lugalzaggisi the loud
Tyrant of Erech and Umma.

II

Lights are moving
On domed hills
Where little monks
Get up in the dark.

Though wild volcanoes
Growl in their sleep
At a green world,
Inside their cloisters

They sit translating
A vision into
The vulgar lingo
of armed cities,

Where brides arrive
Through great doors,
And robbers' bones
Dangle from gallows.

III

Bending forward
With stern faces,
Pilgrims puff
Up the steep bank
In huge hats.

Shouting I run
In the other direction,
Cheerful, unchaste,
With open shirt
And tinkling guitar.

IN PRAISE OF LIMESTONE

If it form the one landscape that we the inconstant ones
    Are consistently homesick for, this is chiefly
Because it dissolves in water. Mark these rounded slopes
    With their surface fragrance of thyme and beneath
A secret system of caves and conduits; hear these springs
    That spurt out everywhere with a chuckle
Each filling a private pool for its fish and carving
    Its own little ravine whose cliffs entertain
The butterfly and the lizard; examine this region
    Of short distances and definite places:

What could be more like Mother or a fitter background
   For her son, the flirtatious male who lounges
Against a rock in the sunlight, never doubting
   That for all his faults he is loved; whose works are but
Extensions of his power to charm? From weathered outcrop
   To hill-top temple, from appearing waters to
Conspicuous fountains, from a wild to a formal vineyard,
   Are ingenious but short steps that a child's wish
To receive more attention than his brothers, whether
   By pleasing or teasing, can easily take.

Watch, then, the band of rivals as they climb up and down
   Their steep stone gennels in twos and threes, sometimes
Arm in arm, but never, thank God, in step; or engaged
   On the shady side of a square at midday in
Voluble discourse, knowing each other too well to think
   There are any important secrets, unable
To conceive a god whose temper-tantrums are moral
   And not to be pacified by a clever line
Or a good lay: for, accustomed to a stone that responds,
   They have never had to veil their faces in awe
Of a crater whose blazing fury could not be fixed;
   Adjusted to the local needs of valleys
Where everything can be touched or reached by walking,
   Their eyes have never looked into infinite space
Through the lattice-work of a nomad's comb; born lucky,
   Their legs have never encountered the fungi
And insects of the jungle, the monstrous forms and lives
   With which we have nothing, we like to hope, in common.
So, when one of them goes to the bad, the way his mind works
   Remains comprehensible: to become a pimp
Or deal in fake jewellery or ruin a fine tenor voice
   For effects that bring down the house could happen to all
But the best and the worst of us . . .

                       That is why, I suppose,
   The best and worst never stayed here long but sought
Immoderate soils where the beauty was not so external,
   The light less public and the meaning of life

Something more than a mad camp. 'Come!' cried the granite
    wastes,
  'How evasive is your humour, how accidental
Your kindest kiss, how permanent is death.' (Saints-to-be
    Slipped away sighing.) 'Come!' purred the clays and gravels.
'On our plains there is room for armies to drill; rivers
    Wait to be tamed and slaves to construct you a tomb
In the grand manner: soft as the earth is mankind and both
    Need to be altered.' (Intendent Caesars rose and
Left, slamming the door.) But the really reckless were fetched
    By an older colder voice, the oceanic whisper:
'I am the solitude that asks and promises nothing;
    That is how I shall set you free. There is no love;
There are only the various envies, all of them sad.'

    They were right, my dear, all those voices were right
And still are; this land is not the sweet home that it looks,
    Nor its peace the historical calm of a site
Where something was settled once and for all: A backward
    And delapidated province, connected
To the big busy world by a tunnel, with a certain
    Seedy appeal, is that all it is now? Not quite:
It has a worldly duty which in spite of itself
    It does not neglect, but calls into question
All the Great Powers assume; it disturbs our rights. The poet,
    Admired for his earnest habit of calling
The sun the sun, his mind Puzzle, is made uneasy
    By these solid statues which so obviously doubt
His antimythological myth; and these gamins,
    Pursuing the scientist down the tiled colonnade
With such lively offers, rebuke his concern for Nature's
    Remotest aspects: I, too, am reproached, for what
And how much you know. Not to lose time, not to get caught,
    Not to be left behind, not, please! to resemble
The beasts who repeat themselves, or a thing like water
    Or stone whose conduct can be predicted, these
Are our Common Prayer, whose greatest comfort is music
    Which can be made anywhere, is invisible,

And does not smell. In so far as we have to look forward
    To death as a fact, no doubt we are right: but if
Sins can be forgiven, if bodies rise from the dead,
    These modifications of matter into
Innocent athletes and gesticulating fountains,
    Made solely for pleasure, make a further point:
The blessed will not care what angle they are regarded from,
    Having nothing to hide. Dear, I know nothing of
Either, but when I try to imagine a faultless love
    Or the life to come, what I hear is the murmur
Of underground streams, what I see is a limestone landscape.

ONE CIRCUMLOCUTION

Sometimes we see astonishingly clearly
The out-there-when we are already in;
Now that is not what we are here-for really.

All its to-do is bound to re-occur,
Is nothing therefore that we need to say;
How then to make its compromise refer

To what could not be otherwise instead
And has its being as its own to be,
The once-for-all that is not seen nor said?

Tell for the power how to thunderclaps
The graves flew open, the rivers ran up-hill;
Such staged importance is at most perhaps.

S̶p̶e̶a̶k̶ well of moonlight on a winding stair,
Of light-boned children under great green oaks;
The wonder, yes, but death should not be there.

One circumlocution as used as any
Depends, it seems, upon the joke of rhyme
For the pure joy; else why should so many

Poems which make us cry direct us to
Ourselves at our least apt, least kind, least true,
Where a blank I loves blankly a blank You?

THEIR LONELY BETTERS

As I listened from a beach-chair in the shade
To all the noises that my garden made,
It seemed to me only proper that words
Should be withheld from vegetables and birds.

A robin with no Christian name ran through
The Robin-Anthem which was all it knew,
And rustling flowers for some third party waited   *bee*
To say which pairs, if any, should get mated.

Not one of them was capable of lying,
There was not one which knew that it was dying
Or could have with a rhythm or a rhyme
Assumed responsibility for time.

Let them leave language to their lonely betters
Who count some days and long for certain letters;

We, too, make noises when we laugh or weep,
Words are for those with <u>promises to keep.</u> *cf. Frost*

" We look before and after... "

SONG

Deftly, admiral, cast your fly
   Into the slow deep hover,
Till the wise old trout mistake and die;
   Salt are the deeps that cover
   The glittering fleets you led,
     White is your head.

Read on, ambassador, engrossed
   In your favourite Stendhal;
The Outer Provinces are lost,
   Unshaven horsemen swill
   The great wines of the Chateaux
     Where you danced long ago.

Do not turn, do not lift, your eyes
   Toward the still pair standing
On the bridge between your properties,
   Indifferent to your minding:
   In its glory, in its power,
     This is their hour.

Nothing your strength, your skill, could do
   Can alter their embrace
Or dispersuade the Furies who
   At the appointed place
   With claw and dreadful brow
     Wait for them now.

PLEASURE ISLAND

What there is as a surround to our figures
    Is very old, very big,
Very formidable indeed; the ocean
    Stares right past us as though
No one here was worth drowning, and the eye, true
    Blue all summer, of the sky
Would not miss a huddle of huts related
    By planks, a dock, a state
Of undress and improvised abandon
    Upon shadowless sand.
To send a cry of protest or a call for
    Protection up into all
Those dazzling miles, to add, however sincerely,
    One's occasional tear
To that volume, would be rather silly,
    Nor is there one small hill
For the hopeful to climb, one tree for the hopeless
    To sit under and mope;
The coast is a blur and without meaning
    The churches and routines
Which stopped there and never cared or dared to
    Cross over to interfere
With this outpost where nothing is wicked
    But to be sorry or sick,
But one thing unneighbourly, work. Sometimes
    A visitor may come
With notebooks intending to make its quiet
    Emptiness his ally
In accomplishing immortal chapters,
    But the hasty tap-tap-tap
Of his first day becomes by the second
    A sharp spasmodic peck
And by the third is extinct; we find him
    Next improving his mind
On the beach with a book, but the dozing
    Afternoon is opposed

To rhyme and reason and chamber music,
     The plain sun has no use
For the printing press, the wheel, the electric
     Light, and the waves reject
Sympathy: soon he gives in, stops stopping
     To think, lets his book drop
And lies, like us, on his stomach watching
     As bosom, backside, crotch
Or other sacred trophy is borne in triumph
     Past his adoring by
Souls he does not try to like; then, getting
     Up, gives all to the wet
Clasps of the sea or surrenders his scruples
     To some great gross braying group
That will be drunk till Fall. The tide rises
     And falls, our household ice
Drips to death in the dark and our friendships
     Prepare for a weekend
They will probably not survive: for our
     Lenient amusing shore
Knows in fact about all the dyings, is in
     Fact our place, namely this
Place of a skull, a place where the rose of
     Self-punishment will grow.
The sunset happens, the bar is copious
     With fervent life that hopes
To make sense, but down the beach some decaying
     Spirit shambles away,
Kicking idly at driftwood and dead shellfish
     And excusing itself
To itself with evangelical gestures
     For having failed the test:
The moon is up there, but without warning,
     A little before dawn,
Miss Lovely, life and soul of the party,
     Wakes with a dreadful start,
Sure that whatever—O God!—she is in for
     Is about to begin,

Or hearing, beyond the hushabye noises
  Of sea and Me, just a voice
Ask as one might the time or a trifle
  Extra her money and her life.

THE FALL OF ROME

FOR CYRIL CONNOLLY

The piers are pummelled by the waves;
In a lonely field the rain
Lashes an abandoned train;
Outlaws fill the mountain caves.

Fantastic grow the evening gowns;
Agents of the Fisc pursue
Absconding tax-defaulters through
The sewers of provincial towns.

Private rites of magic send
The temple prostitutes to sleep;
All the literati keep
An imaginary friend.

Cerebrotonic Catos may
Extol the Ancient Disciplines,
But the muscle-bound Marines
Mutiny for food and pay.

Caesar's double-bed is warm
As an unimportant clerk
Writes I DO NOT LIKE MY WORK
On a pink official form.

Unendowed with wealth or pity,
Little birds with scarlet legs,
Sitting on their speckled eggs,
Eye each flu-infected city.

Altogether elsewhere, vast
Herds of reindeer move across
Miles and miles of golden moss,
Silently and very fast.

THE MANAGERS

In the bad old days it was not so bad:
    The top of the ladder
Was an amusing place to sit; success
    Meant quite a lot—leisure
And huge meals, more palaces filled with more
    Objects, books, girls, horses
Than one would ever get round to, and to be
    Carried uphill while seeing
Others walk. To rule was a pleasure when
    One wrote a death-sentence
On the back of the Ace of Spades and played on
    With a new deck. Honours
Are not so physical or jolly now,
    For the species of Powers
We are used to are not like that. Could one of them
    Be said to resemble
The Tragic Hero, the Platonic Saint,
    Or would any painter

Portray one rising triumphant from a lake
    On a dolphin, naked,
Protected by an umbrella of cherubs? Can
    They so much as manage
To behave like genuine Caesars when alone
    Or drinking with cronies,
To let their hair down and be frank about
    The world? It is doubtful.
The last word on how we may live or die
    Rests today with such quiet
Men, working too hard in rooms that are too big,
    Reducing to figures
What is the matter, what is to be done.
    A neat little luncheon
Of sandwiches is brought to each on a tray,
    Nourishment they are able
To take with one hand without looking up
    From papers a couple
Of secretaries are needed to file,
    From problems no smiling
Can dismiss; the typewriters never stop
    But whirr like grasshoppers
In the silent siesta heat as, frivolous
    Across their discussions,
From woods unaltered by our wars and our vows
    There drift the scents of flowers
And the songs of birds who will never vote
    Or bother to notice
Those distinguishing marks a lover sees
    By instinct and policemen
Can be trained to observe; far into the night
    Their windows burn brightly
And, behind their backs bent over some report,
    On every quarter,
For ever like a god or a disease
    There on the earth the reason
In all its aspects why they are tired, the weak,
    The inattentive, seeking

Someone to blame; if, to recuperate
    They go a-playing, their greatness
Encounters the bow of the chef or the glance
    Of the ballet-dancer
Who cannot be ruined by any master's fall.
    To rule must be a calling,
It seems, like surgery or sculpture, the fun
    Neither love nor money
But taking necessary risks, the test
    Of one's skill, the question,
If difficult, their own reward. But then
    Perhaps one should mention
Also what must be a comfort as they guess
    In times like the present
When guesses can prove so fatally wrong,
    The fact of belonging
To the very select indeed, to those
    For whom, just supposing
They do, there will be places on the last
    Plane out of disaster.
No; no one is really sorry for their
    Heavy gait and careworn
Look, nor would they thank you if you said you were.

BARBED WIRE

      Across the square,
Between the burnt-out Law Courts and Police Headquarters,
Past the Cathedral far too damaged to repair,
Around the Grand Hotel patched up to hold reporters,

Near huts of some Emergency Committee,
The barbed wire runs through the abolished City.

    Across the plains,
Between two hills, two villages, two trees, two friends,
The barbed wire runs which neither argues nor explains
But where it likes a place, a path, a railroad ends,
    The humour, the cuisine, the rites, the taste,
    The pattern of the City, are erased.

    Across our sleep
The barbed wire also runs: It trips us so we fall
And white ships sail without us though the others weep,
It makes our sorry fig-leaf at the Sneerers' Ball,
    It ties the smiler to the double bed,
    It keeps on growing from the witch's head.

    Behind the wire
Which is behind the mirror, our Image is the same
Awake or dreaming: It has no image to admire,
No age, no sex, no memory, no creed, no name,
    It can be counted, multiplied, employed
    In any place, at any time destroyed.

    Is it our friend?
No; that is our hope; that we weep and It does not grieve,
That for It the wire and the ruins are not the end:
This is the flesh we are but never would believe,
    The flesh we die but it is death to pity;
    This is Adam waiting for His City.

UNDER SIRIUS

Yes, these are the dog-days, Fortunatus:
    The heather lies limp and dead
  On the mountain, the baltering torrent
    Shrunk to a soodling thread;
Rusty the spears of the legion, unshaven its captain,
    Vacant the scholar's brain
    Under his great hat,
  Drug as she may the Sibyl utters
    A gush of table-chat.

And you yourself with a head-cold and upset stomach,
    Lying in bed till noon,
  Your bills unpaid, your much advertised
    Epic not yet begun,
Are a sufferer too. All day, you tell us, you wish
    Some earthquake would astonish
    Or the wind of the Comforter's wing
  Unlock the prisons and translate
    The slipshod gathering.

And last night, you say, you dreamed of that bright blue
        morning,
    The hawthorn hedges in bloom,
  When, serene in their ivory vessels,
    The three wise Maries come,
Sossing through seamless waters, piloted in
    By sea-horse and fluent dolphin:
    Ah! how the cannons roar,
  How jocular the bells as They
    Indulge the peccant shore.

It is natural to hope and pious, of course, to believe
    That all in the end shall be well,
  But first of all, remember,
    So the Sacred Books foretell,
The rotten fruit shall be shaken. Would your hope make sense

If today were that moment of silence
    Before it break and drown
When the insurrected eagre hangs
    Over the sleeping town?

How will you look and what will you do when the basalt
    Tombs of the sorcerers shatter
And their guardian megalopods
    Come after you pitter-patter?
How will you answer when from their qualming spring
    The immortal nymphs fly shrieking
And out of the open sky
    The pantocratic riddle breaks—
    'Who are you and why?'

For when in a carol under the apple-trees
    The reborn featly dance,
There will also, Fortunatus,
    Be those who refused their chance,
Now pottering shades, querulous beside the salt-pits,
    And mawkish in their wits,
    To whom these dull dog-days
    Between event seem crowned with olive
    And golden with self-praise.

NUMBERS AND FACES

The Kingdom of Number is all boundaries
Which may be beautiful and must be true;

To ask if it is big or small proclaims one
The sort of lover who should stick to faces.

Lovers of small numbers go benignly potty,
Believe all tales are thirteen chapters long,
Have animal doubles, carry pentagrams,
Are Millerites, Baconians, Flat-Earth-Men.

Lovers of big numbers go horridly mad,
Would have the Swiss abolished, all of us
Well purged, somatotyped, baptised, taught baseball,
They empty bars, spoil parties, run for Congress.

True, between faces almost any number
Might come in handy, and One is always real;
But which could any face call good, for calling
Infinity a number does not make it one.

A HOUSEHOLD

When, to disarm suspicious minds at lunch
Before coming to the point or at golf,
The bargain driven, to soothe hurt feelings,

He talks about his home, he never speaks
(A reticence for which they all admire him)
Of his bride so worshipped and so early lost.

But proudly tells of that young scamp his heir,
Of black eyes given and received, thrashings
Endured without a sound to save a chum;

Or calls their spotted maleness to revere
His saintly mother, calm and kind and wise,
A grand old lady pouring out the tea.

Whom, though, has he ever asked for the week-end?
Out to his country mansion in the evening,
Another merger signed, he drives alone:

To be avoided by a miserable runt
Who wets his bed and cannot throw or whistle,
A tell-tale, a crybaby, a failure;

To the revilings of a slatternly hag
Who caches bottles in her mattress, spits
And shouts obscenities from the landing;

Worse, to find both in an unholy alliance,
Youth stealing Age the liquor-cupboard key,
Age teaching Youth to lie with a straight face.

Disgraces to keep hidden from the world
Where rivals, envying his energy and brains
And with rattling skeletons of their own,

Would see in him the villain of this household,
Whose bull-voice scared a sensitive young child,
Whose coldness drove a doting parent mad.

Besides, (which might explain why he has neither
Altered his will nor called the doctor in)
He half believes, call it a superstition,

It is for his sake that they hate and fear him:
Should they unmask and show themselves worth loving,
Loving and sane and manly, he would die.

PRECIOUS FIVE

Be patient, solemn nose,
Serve in a world of prose
The present moment well
Nor surlily contrast
Its brash ill-mannered smell
With grand scents of the past;
That calm enchanted wood,
That grave world where you stood
So gravely at its middle,
Its oracle and riddle,
Has all been altered, now
In anxious times you serve
As bridge from mouth to brow,
An asymmetric curve
Thrust outward from a face
Time-conscious into space,
Whose oddness may provoke
To a mind-saving joke
A mind that would it were
An apathetic sphere:
Point, then, for honour's sake
Up the storm-beaten slope
From memory to hope
The way you cannot take.

Be modest, lively ears,
Spoiled darlings of a stage
Where any caper cheers
The paranoiac mind
Of this undisciplined
And concert-going age,
So lacking in conviction
It cannot take pure fiction
And what it wants from you
Are rumours partly true;
Before you catch its sickness

Submit your lucky quickness
And levity to rule,
Go back again to school,
Drudge patiently until
No whisper is too much
And your precision such
At any sound that all
Seem natural, not one
Fantastic or banal,
And then do what you will:
Dance with angelic grace,
In ecstasy and fun,
The luck you cannot place.

Be civil, hands; on you
Although you cannot read
Is written what you do
And blows you struck so blindly
In temper or in greed,
Your tricks of long ago,
Eyes, kindly or unkindly,
Unknown to you will know;
Revere those hairy wrists
And leg-of-mutton fists
Which pulverised the trolls
And carved deep Donts in stone,
Great hands which under knolls
Are now disjointed bone,
But what has been has been;
A tight arthritic claw
Or aldermanic paw
Waving about in praise
Of those homeric days
Is impious and obscene:
Grow, hands, into those living
Hands which true hands should be
By making and by giving
To hands you cannot see.

Look, naked eyes, look straight
At all eyes but your own
Lest in a tête-à-tête
Of glances double-crossed,
Both knowing and both known,
Your nakedness be lost;
Rove curiously about
But look from inside out,
Compare two eyes you meet
By dozens on the street,
One shameless, one ashamed,
Too lifeless to be blamed,
With eyes met now and then
Looking from living men,
Which in petrarchan fashion
Play opposite the heart,
Their humour to her passion,
Her nature to their art,
For mutual undeceiving;
True seeing is believing
(What sight can never prove)
There is a world to see:
Look outward, eyes, and love
Those eyes you cannot be.

Praise, tongue, the Earthly Muse
By number and by name
In any style you choose,
For nimble tongues and lame
Have both found favour; praise
Her port and sudden ways,
Now fish-wife and now queen,
Her reason and unreason:
Though freed from that machine,
Praise Her revolving wheel
Of appetite and season
In honour of Another,
The old self you become

At any drink or meal,
That animal of taste
And of his twin, your brother,
Unlettered, savage, dumb,
Down there below the waist:
Although your style be fumbling,
Half stutter and half song,
Give thanks however bumbling,
Telling of Her dear sake
To whom all styles belong
The truth She cannot make.

Be happy, precious five,
So long as I'm alive
Nor try to ask me what
You should be happy for;
Think, if it helps, of love
Or alcohol or gold,
But do as you are told.
I could (which you cannot)
Find reasons fast enough
To face the sky and roar
In anger and despair
At what is going on,
Demanding that it name
Whoever is to blame:
The sky would only wait
Till all my breath was gone
And then reiterate
As if I wasn't there
That singular command
I do not understand,
Bless what there is for being,
Which has to be obeyed, for
What else am I made for,
Agreeing or disagreeing.

THE SHIELD OF ACHILLES

     She looked over his shoulder
       For vines and olive trees,
     Marble well-governed cities
       And ships upon untamed seas,
     But there on the shining metal
       His hands had put instead
     An artificial wilderness
       And a sky like lead.

A plain without a feature, bare and brown,
   No blade of grass, no sign of neighbourhood,
Nothing to eat and nowhere to sit down,
   Yet, congregated on its blankness, stood
   An unintelligible multitude.
A million eyes, a million boots in line,
Without expression, waiting for a sign.

Out of the air a voice without a face
   Proved by statistics that some cause was just
In tones as dry and level as the place:
   No one was cheered and nothing was discussed;
   Column by column in a cloud of dust
They marched away enduring a belief
Whose logic brought them, somewhere else, to grief.

     She looked over his shoulder
       For ritual pieties,
     White flower-garlanded heifers,
       Libation and sacrifice,
     But there on the shining metal
       Where the altar should have been,
     She saw by his flickering forge-light
       Quite another scene.

Barbed wire enclosed an arbitrary spot
   Where bored officials lounged (one cracked a joke)

And sentries sweated for the day was hot:
    A crowd of ordinary decent folk
    Watched from without and neither moved nor spoke
As three pale figures were led forth and bound
To three posts driven upright in the ground.

The mass and majesty of this world, all
    That carries weight and always weighs the same
Lay in the hands of others; they were small
    And could not hope for help and no help came:
    What their foes liked to do was done, their shame
Was all the worst could wish; they lost their pride
And died as men before their bodies died.

            She looked over his shoulder
                For athletes at their games,
            Men and women in a dance
                Moving their sweet limbs
            Quick, quick, to music,
                But there on the shining shield
            His hands had set no dancing-floor
                But a weed-choked field.

A ragged urchin, aimless and alone,
    Loitered about that vacancy, a bird
Flew up to safety from his well-aimed stone:
    That girls are raped, that two boys knife a third,
    Were axioms to him, who'd never heard
Of any world where promises were kept.
Or one could weep because another wept.

            The thin-lipped armourer,
                Hephaestos hobbled away,
            Thetis of the shining breasts
                Cried out in dismay
            At what the god had wrought
                To please her son, the strong
            Iron-hearted man-slaying Achilles
                Who would not live long.

FLEET VISIT

The sailors come ashore
Out of their hollow ships,
Mild-looking middle class boys
Who read the comic strips;
One baseball game is more
To them than fifty Troys.

They look a bit lost, set down
In this unamerican place
Where natives pass with laws
And futures of their own;
They are not here because
But only just-in-case.

The whore and ne'er-do-well
Who pester them with junk
In their grubby ways at least
Are serving the Social Beast;
They neither make nor sell—
No wonder they get drunk.

But their ships on the dazzling blue
Of this harbour actually gain
From having nothing to do;
Without a human will
To tell them whom to kill
Their structures are humane

And, far from looking lost,
Look as if they were meant
To be pure abstract design
By some master of pattern and line,
Certainly worth every cent
Of the millions they must have cost.

THE WILLOW-WREN AND THE STARE

A starling and a willow-wren
 On a may-tree by a weir
Saw them meet and heard him say;
 'Dearest of my dear,
More lively than these waters chortling
 As they leap the dam,
My sweetest duck, my precious goose,
 My white lascivious lamb.'
With a smile she listened to him,
 Talking to her there:
What does he want? said the willow-wren;
 Much too much, said the stare.

'Forgive these loves who dwell in me,
 These brats of greed and fear,
The honking bottom-pinching clown,
 The snivelling sonneteer,
That so, between us, even these,
 Who till the grave are mine,
For all they fall so short of may,
 Dear heart, be still a sign.'
With a smile she closed her eyes,
 Silent she lay there:
Does he mean what he says? said the willow-wren;
 Some of it, said the stare.

'Hark! Wild Robin winds his horn
 And, as his notes require,
Now our laughter-loving spirits
 Must in awe retire
And let their kinder partners,
 Speechless with desire,
Go in their holy selfishness,
 Unfunny to the fire.'
Smiling, silently she threw
 Her arms about him there:

138

Is it only that? said the willow-wren;
   It's that as well, said the stare.

Waking in her arms he cried,
   Utterly content;
'I have heard the high good noises,
   Promoted for an instant,
Stood upon the shining outskirts
   Of that Joy I thank
For you, my dog and every goody.'
   There on the grass bank
She laughed, he laughed, they laughed together,
   Then they ate and drank:
Did he know what he meant? said the willow-wren—
   God only knows, said the stare.

THE PROOF

'When rites and melodies begin
   To alter modes and times,
And timid bar-flies boast aloud
   Of uncommitted crimes,
And leading families are proud
   To dine with their black sheep,
What promises, what discipline,
   If any, will Love keep?'
     So roared Fire on their right:
       But Tamino and Pamina
       Walked past its rage,
     Sighing O, sighing O,

In timeless fermatas of awe and delight
    (Innocent? Yes. Ignorant? No.)
        Down the grim passage.

'When stinking Chaos lifts the latch,
    And Grotte backward spins,
And Helen's nose becomes a beak
    And cats and dogs grow chins,
And daisies claw and pebbles shriek,
    And Form and Colour part,
What swarming hatreds then will hatch
    Out of Love's riven heart'.
        So hissed Water on their left:
            But Pamina and Tamino
            Opposed its spite,
        With his worship, with her sweetness—
O look now! See how they emerge from the cleft
    (Frightened? No. Happy? Yes.)
        Out into sunlight.

A PERMANENT WAY

Self-drivers may curse their luck,
Stuck on new-fangled trails,
But the good old train will jog
To the dogma of its rails

And steam so straight ahead
That I cannot be led astray
By tempting scenes which occur
Along any permanent way.

Intriguing dales escape
Into hills of the shape I like,
Though, were I actually put
Where a foot-path leaves the pike

For some steep romantic spot,
I should ask what chance there is
Of at least a ten-dollar cheque
Or a family peck of a kiss:

But, forcibly held to my tracks,
I can safely relax and dream
Of a love and a livelihood
To fit that wood or stream;

And what could be greater fun,
Once one has chosen and paid,
Than the inexpensive delight
Of a choice one might have made.

NOCTURNE

Make this night loveable,
Moon, and with eye single
Looking down from up there
Bless me, One especial
And friends everywhere.

With a cloudless brightness
Surround our absences;

Innocent be our sleeps,
Watched by great still spaces,
White hills, glittering deeps.

Parted by circumstance,
Grant each your indulgence
That we may meet in dreams
For talk, for dalliance,
By warm hearths, by cool streams

Shine lest tonight any,
In the dark suddenly,
Wake alone in a bed
To hear his own fury
Wishing his love were dead.

IN MEMORIAM, L.K.A. 1950-1952

At peace under this mandarin sleep, Lucina,
Blue-eyed Queen of white cats: for you the Ischian wave shall
    weep,
When we who now miss you are American dust, and steep
Epomeo in peace and war augustly a grave-watch keep.

WINDS

FOR ALEXIS LEGER

Deep below our violences.
Quite still, lie our First Dad, his watch
   And many little maids,
But the boneless winds that blow
   Round law-court and temple
Recall to Metropolis
   That Pliocene Friday when,
At His holy insufflation
   (Had He picked a teleost
Or an arthropod to inspire,
   Would our death also have come?)
One bubble-brained creature said;
   'I am loved, therefore I am':
And well by now might the lion
   Be lying down with the kid,
Had he stuck to that logic.

Winds make weather; weather
Is what nasty people are
   Nasty about and the nice
Show a common joy in observing:
   When I seek an image
For our Authentic City,
   (Across what brigs of dread,
Down what gloomy galleries,
   Must we stagger or crawl
Before we may cry—O look!?)
   I see old men in hall-ways
Tapping their barometers,
   Or a lawn over which

The first thing after breakfast,
    A paterfamilias
Hurries to inspect his rain-gauge.

Goddess of winds and wisdom,
    When, on some windless day
Of dejection, unable
    To name or to structure,
Your poet with bodily tics,
    Scratching, tapping his teeth,
Tugging the lobe of an ear,
    Unconsciously invokes You,
Show Your good nature, allow
    Rooster or whistling maid
To fetch him Arthur O'Bower;
    Then, if moon-faced Nonsense,
That erudite forger, stalk
    Through the seven kingdoms,
Set Your poplars a-shiver
    To warn Your clerk lest he
Die like an Old Believer
    For some spurious reading:
And in all winds, no matter
    Which of Your twelve he may hear,
Equinox gales at midnight
    Howling through marram grass,
Or a faint susurration
    Of pines on a cloudless
Afternoon in midsummer,
    Let him feel You present,
That every verbal rite
    May be fittingly done,
And done in anamnesis
    Of what is excellent
Yet a visible creature,
    Earth, Sky, a few dear names.

WOODS

FOR NICHOLAS NABAKOV

Sylvan meant savage in those primal woods
Piero di Cosimo so loved to draw,
Where nudes, bears, lions, sows with women's heads
Mounted and murdered and ate each other raw,
Nor thought the lightning-kindled bush to tame
But, flabbergasted, fled the useful flame.

Reduced to patches owned by hunting squires
Of villages with ovens and a stocks,
They whispered still of most unsocial fires,
Though Crown and Mitre warned their silly flocks
The pasture's humdrum rhythms to approve
And to abhor the licence of the grove.

Guilty intention still looks for a hotel
That wants no details and surrenders none;
A wood is that, and throws in charm as well,
And many a semi-innocent, undone,
Has blamed its nightingales who round the deed
Sang with such sweetness of a happy greed.

Those birds, of course, did nothing of the sort,
And, as for sylvan nature, if you take
A snapshot at a picnic, O how short
And lower-ordersy the Gang will look
By those vast lives that never took another
And are not scared of gods, ghosts, or stepmother.

Among these coffins of its by-and-by
The Public can (it cannot on a coast)
Bridle its skirt-and-bargain-chasing eye,
And where should an austere philologist
Relax but in the very world of shade
From which the matter of his field was made.

Old sounds re-educate an ear grown coarse,
As Pan's green father suddenly raps out
A burst of undecipherable Morse,
And cuckoos mock in Welsh, and doves create
In rustic English over all they do
To rear their modern family of two.

Now here, now there, some loosened element,
A fruit in vigour or a dying leaf,
Utters its private idiom for descent,
And late man, listening through his latter grief,
Hears, close or far, the oldest of his joys,
Exactly as it was, the water noise.

A well-kempt forest begs Our Lady's grace;
Someone is not disgusted, or at least
Is laying bets upon the human race
Retaining enough decency to last;
The trees encountered on a country stroll
Reveal a lot about a country's soul.

A small grove massacred to the last ash,
An oak with heart-rot, give away the show:
This great society is going smash;
They cannot fool us with how fast they go,
How much they cost each other and the gods!
A culture is no better than its woods.

MOUNTAINS

FOR HEDWIG PETZOLD

I know a retired dentist who only paints mountains,
    But the Masters seldom care
That much, who sketch them in beyond a holy face
    Or a highly dangerous chair;
While a normal eye perceives them as a wall
Between worse and better, like a child, scolded in France,
Who wishes he were crying on the Italian side of the Alps:
        Caesar does not rejoice when high ground
            Makes a darker map,
        Nor does Madam. Why should they? A serious being
            Cries out for a gap.

And it is curious how often in steep places
    You meet someone short who frowns,
A type you catch beheading daisies with a stick:
    Small crooks flourish in big towns,
But perfect monsters—remember Dracula—
Are bred on crags in castles; those unsmiling parties,
Clumping off at dawn in the gear of their mystery
        For points up, are a bit alarming;
            They have the balance, nerve,
        And habit of the Spiritual, but what God
            Does their Order serve?

A civil man is a citizen. Am I
    To see in the Lake District, then,
Another bourgeois invention like the piano?
    Well, I won't. How can I, when
I wish I stood now on a platform at Penrith,
Zurich, or any junction at which you leave the express
For a local that swerves off soon into a cutting? Soon
        Tunnels begin, red farms disappear,
            Hedges turn to walls,
        Cows become sheep, you smell peat or pinewood, you hear
            Your first waterfalls,

And what looked like a wall turns out to be a world
    With measurements of its own
And a style of gossip. To manage the Flesh,
    When angels of ice and stone
Stand over her day and night who make it so plain
They detest any kind of growth, does not encourage
Euphemisms for the effort: here wayside crucifixes
    Bear witness to a physical outrage,
        And serenades too
Stick to bare fact: 'O my girl has a goitre,
    I've a hole in my shoe!'

Dour. Still, a fine refuge. That boy behind his goats
    Has the round skull of a clan
That fled with bronze before a tougher metal.
    And that quiet old gentleman
With a cheap room at the Black Eagle used to own
Three papers but is not received in Society now:
These farms can always see a panting government coming;
    I'm nordic myself, but even so
        I'd much rather stay
Where the nearest person who could have me hung is
    Some ridges away.

To be sitting in privacy, like a cat
    On the warm roof of a loft,
Where the high-spirited son of some gloomy tarn
    Comes sprinting down through a green croft,
Bright with flowers laid out in exquisite splodges
Like a Chinese poem, while, near enough, a real darling
Is cooking a delicious lunch, would keep me happy for
    What? Five minutes? For an uncatlike
        Creature who has gone wrong,
Five minutes on even the nicest mountain
    Is awfully long.

LAKES

FOR ISAIAH BERLIN

A lake allows an average father, walking slowly,
    To circumvent it in an afternoon,
And any healthy mother to halloo the children
    Back to her bedtime from their games across:
(Anything bigger than that, like Michigan or Baikal,
    Though potable, is an 'estranging sea').

Lake-folk require no fiend to keep them on their toes;
    They leave aggression to ill-bred romantics
Who duel with their shadows over blasted heaths:
    A month in a lacustrine atmosphere
Would find the fluvial rivals waltzing not exchanging
    The rhyming insults of their great-great-uncles.

No wonder Christendom did not get really started
    Till, scarred by torture, white from caves and jails,
Her pensive chiefs converged on the Ascanian Lake
    And by that stork-infested shore invented
The life of Godhead, making catholic the figure
    Of three small fishes in a triangle.

Sly Foreign Ministers should always meet beside one,
    For, whether they walk widdershins or deasil,
The path will yoke their shoulders to one liquid centre
    Like two old donkeys pumping as they plod;
Such physical compassion may not guarantee
    A marriage for their armies, but it helps.

Only a very wicked or conceited man,
    About to sink somewhere in mid-Atlantic,
Could think Poseidon's frown was meant for him in person,
    But it is only human to believe
The little lady of the glacier lake has fallen
    In love with the rare bather whom she drowns.

149

The drinking water of the city where one panics
    At nothing noticing how real one is
May come from reservoirs whose guards are all too conscious
    Of being followed: Webster's cardinal
Saw in a fish-pool something horrid with a hay-rake;
    I know a Sussex hammer-pond like that.

A haunted lake is sick, though; normally, they doctor
    Our tactile fevers with a visual world
Where beaks are dumb like boughs and faces safe like houses;
    The water-scorpion finds it quite unticklish,
And, if it shudder slightly when caressed by boats,
    It never asks for water or a loan.

Liking one's Nature, as lake-lovers do, benign
    Goes with a wish for savage dogs and man-traps:
One Fall, one dispossession, is enough I'm sorry;
    Why should I give Lake Eden to the Nation
Just because every mortal Jack and Jill has been
    The genius of some amniotic mere?

It is unlikely I shall ever keep a swan
    Or build a tower on any small tombolo,
But that's not going to stop me wondering what sort
    Of lake I would decide on if I should.
Moraine, pot, oxbow, glint, sink, crater, piedmont, dimple . . . ?
    Just reeling off their names is ever so comfy.

ISLANDS

FOR GIOCONDO SACCHETTI

Old saints on millstones float with cats
    To islands out at sea

Whereon no female pelvis can
   Threaten there agape.

Beyond the long arm of the Law,
   Close to a shipping road,
Pirates in their island lairs
   Observe the pirate code.

Obsession with security
   In Sovereigns prevails;
His Highness and The People both
   Pick islands for their jails.

Once, where detected worldlings now
   Do penitential jobs,
Exterminated species played
   Who had not read their Hobbes.

His continental damage done,
   Laid on an island shelf,
Napoleon has five years more
   To talk about himself.

How fascinating is that class
   Whose only member is Me!
Sappho, Tiberius and I
   Hold forth beside the sea.

What is cosier than the shore
   Of a lake turned inside out?
How do all these other people
   Dare to be about?

In democratic nudity
   Their sexes lie; except
By age or weight you could not tell
   The keeping from the kept.

They go, she goes, thou goest, I go
  To a mainland livelihood:
Farmer and fisherman complain
  The other has it good.

PLAINS

FOR WENDELL JOHNSON

I can imagine quite easily ending up
  In a decaying port on a desolate coast,
Cadging drinks from the unwary, a quarrelsome,
  Disreputable old man; I can picture
A second childhood in a valley, scribbling
  Reams of edifying and unreadable verse;
But I cannot see a plain without a shudder:
  'O God, please, please, don't ever make me live there!'

It's horrible to think what peaks come down to,
  That pecking rain and squelching glacier defeat
Tall pomps of stone where goddesses lay sleeping,
  Dreaming of being woken by some chisel's kiss,
That what those blind brutes leave when they are through is
    nothing
  But a mere substance, a clay that meekly takes
The potter's cuff, a gravel that as concrete
  Will unsex any space which it encloses.

And think of growing where all elsewheres are equal!
  So long as there's a hill-ridge somewhere the dreamer
Can place his land of marvels; in poor valleys
  Orphans can head downstream to seek a million:

Here nothing points; to choose between Art and Science
    An embryo genius would have to spin a stick.
What could these farms do if set loose but drift like clouds,
    What goal of unrest is there but the Navy?

Romance? Not in this weather. Ovid's charmer
    Who leads the quadrilles in Arcady, boy-lord
Of hearts who can call their Yes and No their own,
    Would, madcap that he is, soon die of cold or sunstroke:
These lives are in firmer hands; that old grim She
    Who makes the blind dates for the hatless genera
Creates their country matters. (Woe to the child-bed,
    Woe to the strawberries if She's in Her moods!)

And on these attend, greedy as fowl and harsher
    Than any climate, Caesar with all his They.
If a tax-collector disappear in the hills,
    If, now and then, a keeper is shot in the forest,
No thunder follows, but where roads run level,
    How swift to the point of protest strides the Crown.
It hangs, it flogs, it fines, it goes. There is drink.
    There are wives to beat. But Zeus is with the strong.

Born as a rule in some small place (an island,
    Quite often, where a smart lad can spot the bluff
Whence cannon would put the harbour at his mercy),
    Though it is here they chamber with Clio. At this brook
The Christian cross-bow stopped the Heathen scimitar;
    Here is a windmill whence an emperor saw
His right wing crumple; across these cabbage fields
    A pretender's Light Horse made their final charge.

If I were a plainsman I should hate us all,
    From the mechanic rioting for a cheap loaf
To the fastidious palate, hate the painter
    Who steals my wrinkles for his Twelve Apostles,
Hate the priest who cannot even make it shower.
    What could I smile at as I trudged behind my harrow

But bloodshot images of rivers screaming,
  Marbles in panic, and Don't-Care made to care?

As it is, though, I know them personally
  Only as a landscape common to two nightmares:
Across them, spotted by spiders from afar,
  I have tried to run, knowing there was no hiding and no help;
On them, in brilliant moonlight, I have lost my way
  And stood without a shadow at the dead centre
Of an abominable desolation,
  Like Tarquin ravished by his post-coital sadness.

Which goes to show I've reason to be frightened
  Not of plains, of course, but of me. I should like
—Who wouldn't?—to shoot beautifully and be obeyed,
  (I should also like to own a cave with two exits);
I wish I weren't so silly. Though I can't pretend
  To think these flats poetic, it's as well at times
To be reminded that nothing is lovely,
  Not even in poetry, which is not the case.

STREAMS

FOR ELIZABETH DREW

Dear water, clear water, playful in all your streams,
As you dash or loiter through life who does not love
    To sit beside you, to hear you and see you,
  Pure being, perfect in music and movement?

Air is boastful at times, earth slovenly, fire rude,
But you in your bearing are always immaculate,

The most well-spoken of all the older
Servants in the household of Mrs. Nature.

Nobody suspects you of mocking him, for you still
Use the same vocables you were using the day
     Before that unexpected row which
   Downed every hod on half-finished Babel,

And still talk to yourself: nowhere are you disliked;
Arching your torso, you dive from a basalt sill,
     Canter across white chalk, slog forward
   Through red marls, the aboriginal pilgrim,

At home in all sections, but for whom we should be
Idolaters of a single rock, kept apart
     By our landscapes, excluding as alien
   The tales and diets of all other strata.

How could we love the absent one if you did not keep
Coming from a distance, or quite directly assist,
     As when past Iseult's tower you floated
   The willow pash-notes of wanted Tristram?

And *Homo Ludens,* surely, is your child, who make
Fun of our feuds by opposing identical banks,
     Transferring the loam from Huppim
   To Muppim and back each time you crankle.

Growth cannot add to your song: as unchristened brooks
Already you whisper to ants what, as Brahma's son,
     Descending his titanic staircase
   Into Assam, to Himalayan bears you thunder.

And not even man can spoil you: his company
Coarsens roses and dogs but, should he herd you through **a**
     sluice
   To toil at a turbine, or keep you
   Leaping in gardens for his amusement,

Innocent still is your outcry, water, and there
Even, to his soiled heart raging at what it is,
    Tells of a sort of world, quite other,
   Altogether different from this one

With its envies and passports, a polis like that
To which, in the name of scholars everywhere,
    Gaston Paris pledged his allegiance
   As Bismarck's siege-guns came within earshot.

Lately, in that dale of all Yorkshire's the loveliest,
Where, off its fell-side helter-skelter, Kisdon Beck
    Jumps into Swale with a boyish shouting,
   Sprawled out on grass, I dozed for a second,

And found myself following a croquet tournament
In a calm enclosure, with thrushes popular:
    Of all the players in that cool valley
   The best with the mallet was my darling.

While, on the wolds that begirdled it, wild old men
Hunted with spades and hammers, monomaniac each,
    For a megalith or a fossil,
   And bird-watchers stalked the mossy beech-woods.

Suddenly, over the lawn we started to run
For, lo, through the trees in a cream and golden coach
    Drawn by two baby locomotives,
   The god of mortal doting approached us,

Flanked by his bodyguard, those hairy armigers in green
Who laugh at thunderstorms and weep at a blue sky:
    He thanked us for our cheers of homage,
   And promised X and Y a passion undying.

With a wave of his torch he commanded a dance;
So round in a ring we flew, my dear on my right,
    When I awoke. But fortunate seemed that
   Day because of my dream and enlightened,

156

And dearer, water, than ever your voice, as if
Glad—though goodness knows why—to run with the human
   race,
     Wishing, I thought, the least of men their
   Figures of splendour, their holy places.

HORAE CANONICAE

IMMOLATUS VICERIT

PRIME

Simultaneously, as soundlessly,
   Spontaneously, suddenly
As, at the vaunt of the dawn, the kind
   Gates of the body fly open
To its world beyond, the gates of the mind,
   The horn gate and the ivory gate
Swing to, swing shut, instantaneously
   Quell the nocturnal rummage
Of its rebellious fronde, ill-favored,
   Ill-natured and second-rate,
Disenfranchised, widowed and orphaned
   By an historical mistake:
Recalled from the shades to be a seeing being,
   From absence to be on display,
Without a name or history I wake
   Between my body and the day.

Holy this moment, wholly in the right,
   As, in complete obedience

To the light's laconic outcry, next
　　As a sheet, near as a wall,
Out there as a mountain's poise of stone,
　　The world is present, about,
And I know that I am, here, not alone
　　But with a world and rejoice
Unvexed, for the will has still to claim
　　This adjacent arm as my own,
The memory to name me, resume
　　Its routine of praise and blame
And smiling to me is this instant while
　　Still the day is intact, and I
The Adam sinless in our beginning,
　　Adam still previous to any act.

I draw breath; this is of course to wish
　　No matter what, to be wise,
To be different, to die and the cost,
　　No matter how, is Paradise
Lost of course and myself owing a death:
　　The eager ridge, the steady sea,
The flat roofs of the fishing village
　　Still asleep in its bunny,
Though as fresh and sunny still are not friends
　　But things to hand, this ready flesh
No honest equal, but my accomplice now
　　My assassin to be, and my name
Stands for my historical share of care
　　For a lying self-made city,
Afraid of our living task, the dying
　　Which the coming day will ask.

TERCE

After shaking paws with his dog,
(Whose bark would tell the world that he is always kind,)
   The hangman sets off briskly over the heath;
He does not know yet who will be provided
   To do the high works of Justice with:
Gently closing the door of his wife's bedroom,
   (Today she has one of her headaches)
With a sigh the judge descends his marble stair;
   He does not know by what sentence
He will apply on earth the Law that rules the stars:
   And the poet, taking a breather
Round his garden before starting his eclogue,
   Does not know whose Truth he will tell.

Sprites of hearth and store-room, godlings
Of professional mysteries, the Big Ones
   Who can annihilate a city,
Cannot be bothered with this moment: we are left,
   Each to his secret cult, now each of us
Prays to an image of his image of himself:
   'Let me get through this coming day
Without a dressing down from a superior,
   Being worsted in a repartee,
Or behaving like an ass in front of the girls;
   Let something exciting happen,
Let me find a lucky coin on a sidewalk.
   Let me hear a new funny story.'

At this hour we all might be anyone:
It is only our victim who is without a wish
   Who knows already (that is what
We can never forgive. If he knows the answers,
   Then why are we here, why is there even dust?)
Knows already that, in fact, our prayers are heard,
   That not one of us will slip up,

That the machinery of our world will function
   Without a hitch, that today, for once,
There will be no squabbling on Mount Olympus,
   No Chthonian mutters of unrest,
But no other miracle, knows that by sundown
   We shall have had a good Friday.

SEXT

I

You need not see what someone is doing
to know if it is his vocation,

you have only to watch his eyes:
a cook mixing a sauce, a surgeon

making a primary incision,
a clerk completing a bill of lading,

wear the same rapt expression,
forgetting themselves in a function.

How beautiful it is,
that eye-on-the-object look.

To ignore the appetitive goddesses,
to desert the formidable shrines

of Rhea, Aphrodite, Demeter, Diana,
to pray instead to St Phocas,

160

St Barbara, San Saturnino,
or whoever one's patron is,

that one may be worthy of their mystery,
what a prodigious step to have taken.

There should be monuments, there should be odes,
to the nameless heroes who took it first,

to the first flaker of flints
who forgot his dinner,

the first collector of sea-shells
to remain celibate.

Where should we be but for them?
Feral still, un-housetrained, still

wandering through forests without
a consonant to our names,

slaves of Dame Kind, lacking
all notion of a city

and, at this noon, for this death,
there would be no agents.

II

You need not hear what orders he is giving
to know if someone has authority,

you have only to watch his mouth:
when a besieging general sees

a city wall breached by his troops,
when a bacteriologist

realizes in a flash what was wrong
with his hypothesis when,

from a glance at the jury, the prosecutor
knows the defendant will hang,

their lips and the lines around them
relax, assuming an expression

not of simple pleasure at getting
their own sweet way but of satisfaction

at being right, an incarnation
of *Fortitudo, Justicia, Nous.*

You may not like them much
(Who does?) but we owe them

basilicas, divas,
dictionaries, pastoral verse,

the courtesies of the city:
without these judicial mouths

(which belong for the most part
to very great scoundrels)

how squalid existence would be,
tethered for life to some hut village,

afraid of the local snake
or the local ford demon,

speaking the local patois
of some three hundred words

(think of the family squabbles and the
poison-pens, think of the inbreeding)

and, at this noon, there would be no authority
to command this death.

III

Anywhere you like, somewhere
on broad-chested life-giving Earth,

anywhere between her thirstlands
and undrinkable Ocean,

the crowd stands perfectly still,
its eyes (which seem one) and its mouths

(which seem infinitely many)
expressionless, perfectly blank.

The crowd does not see (what everyone sees)
a boxing match, a train wreck,

a battleship being launched,
does not wonder (as everyone wonders)

who will win, what flag she will fly,
how many will be burned alive,

is never distracted
(as everyone is always distracted)

by a barking dog, a smell of fish,
a mosquito on a bald head:

the crowd sees only one thing
(which only the crowd can see)

an epiphany of that
which does whatever is done.

Whatever god a person believes in,
in whatever way he believes,

(no two are exactly alike)
as one of the crowd he believes

and only believes in that
in which there is only one way of believing.

Few people accept each other and most
will never do anything properly,

but the crowd rejects no one, joining the crowd
is the only thing all men can do.

Only because of that can we say
all men are our brothers,

superior, because of that,
to the social exoskeletons: When

have they ever ignored their queens,
for one second stopped work

on their provincial cities, to worship
The Prince of this world like us,

at this noon, on this hill,
in the occasion of this dying.

NONES

What we know to be not possible,
   Though time after time foretold

By wild hermits, by shaman and sybil
  Gibbering in their trances,
Or revealed to a child in some chance rhyme
  Like *will* and *kill*, comes to pass
Before we realize it: we are surprised
  At the ease and speed of our deed
And uneasy: It is barely three,
  Mid-afternoon, yet the blood
Of our sacrifice is already
  Dry on the grass; we are not prepared
For silence so sudden and so soon;
  The day is too hot, too bright, too still,
Too ever, the dead remains too nothing.
  What shall we do till nightfall?

The wind has dropped and we have lost our public.
  The faceless many who always
Collect when any world is to be wrecked,
  Blown up, burnt down, cracked open,
Felled, sawn in two, hacked through, torn apart,
  Have all melted away: not one
Of these who in the shade of walls and trees
  Lie sprawled now, calmly sleeping,
Harmless as sheep, can remember why
  He shouted or what about
So loudly in the sunshine this morning;
  All if challenged would reply
—'It was a monster with one red eye,
  A crowd that saw him die, not I.'—
The hangman has gone to wash, the soldiers to eat;
  We are left alone with our feat.

The Madonna with the green woodpecker,
  The Madonna of the fig-tree,
The Madonna beside the yellow dam,
  Turn their kind faces from us
And our projects under construction,
  Look only in one direction,

Fix their gaze on our completed work:
  Pile-driver, concrete-mixer,
Crane and pick-axe wait to be used again,
  But how can we repeat this?
Outliving our act, we stand where we are,
  As disregarded as some
Discarded artifact of our own,
  Like torn gloves, rusted kettles,
Abandoned branch-lines, worn lop-sided
  Grindstones buried in nettles.

This mutilated flesh, our victim,
  Explains too nakedly, too well,
The spell of the asparagus garden,
  The aim of our chalk-pit game; stamps,
Birds' eggs are not the same, behind the wonder
  Of tow-paths and sunken lanes,
Behind the rapture on the spiral stair,
  We shall always now be aware
Of the deed into which they lead, under
  The mock chase and mock capture,
The racing and tussling and splashing,
  The panting and the laughter,
Be listening for the cry and stillness
  To follow after: wherever
The sun shines, brooks run, books are written,
  There will also be this death.

Soon cool tramontana will stir the leaves,
  The shops will re-open at four,
The empty blue bus in the empty pink square
  Fill up and depart: we have time
To misrepresent, excuse, deny,
  Mythify, use this event
While, under a hotel bed, in prison,
  Down wrong turnings, its meaning
Waits for our lives: sooner than we would choose
  Bread will melt, water will burn,

And the great quell begin, Abaddon
   Set up his triple gallows
At our seven gates, fat Belial make
   Our wives waltz naked; meanwhile
It would be best to go home, if we have a home,
   In any case good to rest.

That our dreaming wills may seem to escape
   This dead calm, wander instead
On knife edges, on black and white squares,
   Across moss, baize, velvet, boards,
Over cracks and hillocks, in mazes
   Of string and penitent cones,
Down granite ramps and damp passages,
   Through gates that will not relatch
And doors marked *Private*, pursued by Moors
   And watched by latent robbers,
To hostile villages at the heads of fjords,
   To dark chateaux where wind sobs
In the pine-trees and telephones ring,
   Inviting trouble, to a room,
Lit by one weak bulb, where our Double sits
   Writing and does not look up.

That, while we are thus away, our own wronged flesh
   May work undisturbed, restoring
The order we try to destroy, the rhythm
   We spoil out of spite: valves close
And open exactly, glands secrete,
   Vessels contract and expand
At the right moment, essential fluids
   Flow to renew exhausted cells,
Not knowing quite what has happened, but awed
   By death like all the creatures
Now watching this spot, like the hawk looking down
   Without blinking, the smug hens
Passing close by in their pecking order,
   The bug whose view is balked by grass.

Or the deer who shyly from afar
  Peer through chinks in the forest.

VESPERS

If the hill overlooking our city has always been known as
Adam's Grave, only at dusk can you see the recumbent giant,
his head turned to the west, his right arm resting for ever on
Eve's haunch

  can you learn, from the way he looks up at the scandalous
pair, what a citizen really thinks of his citizenship,

  just as now you can hear in a drunkard's caterwaul his
rebel sorrows crying for a parental discipline, in lustful eyes
perceive a disconsolate soul, scanning with desperation all passing limbs for some vestige of her faceless angel who in that
long ago when wishing was a help mounted her once and vanished:

  For Sun and Moon supply their conforming masks, but in
this hour of civil twilight all must wear their own faces.

  And it is now that our two paths cross.

  Both simultaneously recognise his Anti-type: that I am an
Arcadian, that he is a Utopian.

  He notes, with contempt, my Aquarian belly: I note, with
alarm, his Scorpion's mouth.

  He would like to see me cleaning latrines: I would like to
see him removed to some other planet.

  Neither speaks. What experience could we possibly share?

  Glancing at a lampshade in a store window, I observe it is
too hideous for anyone in their senses to buy: He observes it is
too expensive for a peasant to buy.

Passing a slum child with rickets, I look the other way: He looks the other way if he passes a chubby one.

I hope our senators will behave like saints, provided they don't reform me: He hopes they will behave like *baritoni cattivi,* and, when lights burn late in the Citadel, I (who have never seen the inside of a police station) am shocked and think: 'Were the city as free as they say, after sundown all her bureaus would be huge black stones':

He (who has been beaten up several times) is not shocked at all but thinks: 'One fine night our boys will be working up there.'

You can see, then, why, between my Eden and his New Jerusalem, no treaty is negotiable.

In my Eden a person who dislikes Bellini has the good manners not to get born: In his New Jerusalem a person who dislikes work will be very sorry he was born.

In my Eden we have a few beam-engines, saddle-tank loco-motives, overshot waterwheels and other beautiful pieces of obsolete machinery to play with: In his New Jerusalem even chefs will be cucumber-cool machine minders.

In my Eden our only source of political news is gossip: In his New Jerusalem there will be a special daily in simplified spelling for non-verbal types.

In my Eden each observes his compulsive rituals and super-stitious tabus but we have no morals: In his New Jerusalem the temples will be empty but all will practise the rational virtues.

One reason for his contempt is that I have only to close my eyes, cross the iron footbridge to the tow-path, take the barge through the short brick tunnel and there I stand in Eden again, welcomed back by the krumhorns, doppions, sordumes of jolly miners and a bob major from the Cathedral (roman-esque) of St Sophie (*Die Kalte*):

One reason for my alarm is that, when he closes his eyes, he arrives, not in New Jerusalem, but on some august day of outrage when hellikins cavort through ruined drawing-rooms and fish-wives intervene in the Chamber or

some autumn night of delations and noyades when the unrepentant thieves (including me) are sequestered and those he hates shall hate themselves instead.

So with a passing glance we take the other's posture; already our steps recede, heading, incorrigible each, towards his kind of meal and evening.

Was it (as it must look to any god of cross-roads) simply a fortuitous intersection of life-paths, loyal to different fibs

or also a rendezvous between accomplices who, in spite of themselves, cannot resist meeting

to remind the other (do both, at bottom, desire truth?) of that half of their secret which he would most like to forget

forcing us both, for a fraction of a second, to remember our victim (but for him I could forget the blood, but for me he could forget the innocence)

on whose immolation (call him Abel, Remus, whom you will, it is one Sin Offering) arcadias, utopias, our dear old bag of a democracy, are alike founded:

For without a cement of blood (it must be human, it must be innocent) no secular wall will safely stand.

COMPLINE

Now, as desire and the things desired
    Cease to require attention,
As, seizing its chance, the body escapes,
    Section by section, to join
Plants in their chaster peace which is more
    To its real taste, now a day is its past,
Its last deed and feeling in, should come
    The instant of recollection

When the whole thing makes sense: it comes, but all
   I recall are doors banging,
Two housewives scolding, an old man gobbling,
   A child's wild look of envy,
Actions, words, that could fit any tale,
   And I fail to see either plot
Or meaning; I cannot remember
   A thing between noon and three.

Nothing is with me now but a sound,
   A heart's rhythm, a sense of stars
Leisurely walking around, and both
   Talk a language of motion
I can measure but not read: maybe
   My heart is confessing her part
In what happened to us from noon till three,
   That constellations indeed
Sing of some hilarity beyond
   All liking and happening,
But, knowing I neither know what they know
   Nor what I ought to know, scorning
All vain fornications of fancy,
   Now let me, blessing them both
For the sweetness of their cassations,
   Accept our separations.

A stride from now will take me into dream,
   Leave me, without a status,
Among its unwashed tribes of wishes
   Who have no dances and no jokes
But a magic cult to propitiate
   What happens from noon till three,
Odd rites which they hide from me—should I chance,
   Say, on youths in an oak-wood
Insulting a white deer, bribes nor threats
   Will get them to blab—and then
Past untruth is one step to nothing,
   For the end, for me as for cities,

171

Is total absence: what comes to be
   Must go back into non-being
For the sake of the equity, the rhythm
   Past measure or comprehending.

Can poets (can men in television)
   Be saved? It is not easy
To believe in unknowable justice
   Or pray in the name of a love
Whose name one's forgotten: *libera*
   Me, libera C (dear C)
      And all poor s-o-b's who never
         Do anything properly, spare
      Us in the youngest day when all are
         Shaken awake, facts are facts,
      (And I shall know exactly what happened
         Today between noon and three)
      That we, too, may come to the picnic
         With nothing to hide, join the dance
      As it moves in perichoresis,
         Turns about the abiding tree.

LAUDS

Among the leaves the small birds sing;
The crow of the cock commands awaking:
In solitude, for company.

Bright shines the sun on creatures mortal;
Men of their neighbours become sensible:
In solitude, for company.

The crow of the cock commands awaking;
Already the mass-bell goes dong-ding:
In solitude, for company.

Men of their neighbours become sensible;
God bless the Realm, God bless the People:
In solitude, for company.

Already the mass-bell goes dong-ding;
The dripping mill-wheel is again turning:
In solitude, for company.

God bless the Realm, God bless the People;
God bless this green world temporal:
In solitude, for company.

The dripping mill-wheel is again turning;
Among the leaves the small birds sing:
In solitude, for company.

METALOGUE TO THE MAGIC FLUTE

(*Lines composed in commemoration of the Mozart Bicentenary, 1956. To be spoken by the singer playing the role of Sarastro.*)

Relax, Maestro, put your baton down:
Only the fogiest of the old will frown
If you the trials of the *Prince* prorogue
To let *Sarastro* speak this Metalogue,
A form acceptable to us, although

Unclassed by *Aristotle* or *Boileau*.
No modern audience finds it incorrect,
For interruption is what we expect
Since that new god, the Paid Announcer, rose,
Who with his quasi-Ossianic prose
Cuts in upon the lovers, halts the band,
To name a sponsor or to praise a brand.
Not that I have a product to describe
That you could wear or cook with or imbibe;
You cannot hoard or waste a work of art:
I come to praise but not to sell *Mozart,*
Who came into this world of war and woe
At Salzburg just two centuries ago,
When kings were many and machines were few
And open Atheism something new.
(It makes a servantless New Yorker sore
To think sheer Genius had to stand before
A mere Archbishop with uncovered head:
But *Mozart* never had to make his bed.)

The history of Music as of Man
Will not go cancrizans, and no ear can
Recall what, when the Archduke *Francis* reigned,
Was heard by ears whose treasure-hoard contained
A *Flute* already but as yet no *Ring;*
Each age has its own mode of listening.
We know the *Mozart* of our fathers' time
Was gay, rococo, sweet, but not sublime,
A Viennese Italian; that is changed
Since music critics learned to feel 'estranged';
Now it's the Germans he is classed amongst,
A *Geist* whose music was composed from *Angst,*
At International Festivals enjoys
An equal status with the Twelve-Tone Boys;
He awes the lovely and the very rich,
And even those *Divertimenti* which
He wrote to play while bottles were uncorked,

Milord chewed noisily, Milady talked,
Are heard in solemn silence, score on knees,
Like quartets by the deafest of the *B*'s.
What next? One can no more imagine how,
In concert halls two hundred years from now,
When the mozartian sound-waves move the air,
The cognoscenti will be moved, than dare
Predict how high orchestral pitch will go,
How many tones will constitute a row,
The tempo at which regimented feet
Will march about the Moon, the form of Suite
For Piano in a Post-Atomic Age,
Prepared by some contemporary *Cage*.

An opera composer may be vexed
By later umbrage taken at his text:
Even *Macaulay*'s schoolboy knows to-day
What *Robert Graves* or *Margaret Mead* would say
About the status of the sexes in this play,
Writ in that era of barbaric dark
'Twixt Modern Mom and Bronze-Age Matriarch.
Where now the Roman Fathers and their creed?
'Ah, where,' sighs *Mr. Mitty*, 'where indeed?',
And glances sideways at his vital spouse
Whose rigid jaw-line and contracted brows
Express her scorn and utter detestation
For Roman views of Female Education.

In Nineteen-Fifty-Six we find the *Queen*
A highly-paid and most efficient Dean
(Who, as we all know, really runs the College),
Sarastro, tolerated for his knowledge,
Teaching the History of Ancient Myth
At *Bryn Mawr, Vassar, Bennington* or *Smith;*
Pamina may a *Time* researcher be
To let *Tamino* take his Ph.D.,
Acquiring manly wisdom as he wishes

While changing diapers and doing dishes;
Sweet *Papagena,* when she's time to spare,
Listens to *Mozart* operas on the air,
Though *Papageno,* we are sad to feel,
Prefers the juke-box to the glockenspiel,
And how is—what was easy in the past—
A democratic villain to be cast?
Monostatos must make his bad impression
Without a race, religion or profession.

A work that lasts two hundred years is tough,
And operas, God knows, must stand enough:
What greatness made, small vanities abuse.
What must they not endure? The Diva whose
Fioriture and climactic note
The silly old composer never wrote,
Conductor *X,* that over-rated bore
Who alters tempi and who cuts the score,
Director *Y* who with ingenious wit
Places his wretched singers in the pit
While dancers mime their roles, *Z* the Designer
Who sets the whole thing on an ocean liner,
The girls in shorts, the men in yachting caps;
Yet Genius triumphs over all mishaps,
Survives a greater obstacle than these,
Translation into foreign Operese
(English sopranos are condemned to *languish*
Because our tenors have to hide their *anguish*);
It soothes the *Frank,* it stimulates the *Greek*:
Genius surpasses all things, even Chic.
We who know nothing—which is just as well—
About the future, can, at least, foretell,
Whether they live in air-borne nylon cubes,
Practise group-marriage or are fed through tubes,
That crowds two centuries from now will press
(Absurd their hair, ridiculous their dress)
And pay in currencies, however weird,

To hear *Sarastro* booming through his beard,
Sharp connoisseurs approve if it is clean
The F in alt of the *Nocturnal Queen,*
Some uncouth creature from the *Bronx* amaze
Park Avenue by knowing all the *K*'s.

How seemly, then, to celebrate the birth
Of one who did no harm to our poor earth,
Created masterpieces by the dozen,
Indulged in toilet humour with his cousin,
And had a pauper's funeral in the rain,
The like of whom we shall not see again:
How comely, also, to forgive; we should,
As *Mozart,* were he living, surely would,
Remember kindly *Salieri*'s shade,
Accused of murder and his works unplayed,
Nor, while we praise the dead, should we forget
We have *Stravinsky*—bless him!—with us yet.
{ *Basta!* Maestro, make your minions play!
In all hearts, as in our finale, may
Reason & Love be crowned, assume their rightful sway.

THE SONG

So large a morning so itself to lean
Over so many and such little hills
All at rest in roundness and rigs of green
Can cope with a rebellious wing that wills
To better its obedient double quite
As daring in the lap of any lake
The wind from which ascension puts to flight
Tribes of a beauty which no care can break.

Climbing to song it hopes to make amends
For whiteness drabbed for glory said away
And be immortal after but because
Light upon a valley where its love was
So lacks all picture of reproach it ends
Denying what it started up to say.

GOOD-BYE TO THE MEZZOGIORNO

FOR CARLO IZZO

Out of a gothic North, the pallid children
    Of a potato, beer-or-whisky
Guilt culture, we behave like our fathers and come
    Southward into a sunburnt otherwhere

Of vineyards, baroque, *la bella figura,*
    To these feminine townships where men
Are males, and siblings untrained in a ruthless
    Verbal in-fighting as it is taught

In Protestant rectories upon drizzling
    Sunday afternoons—no more as unwashed
Barbarians out for gold, nor as profiteers
    Hot for Old Masters, but for plunder

Nevertheless—some believing *amore*
    Is better down South and much cheaper
(Which is doubtful), some persuaded exposure
    To strong sunlight is lethal to germs

(Which is patently false) and others, like me,
   In middle-age hoping to twig from
What we are not what we might be next, a question
   The South seems never to raise. Perhaps

A tongue in which Nestor and Apemantus,
   Don Ottavio and Don Giovanni make
Equally beautiful sounds is unequipped
   To frame it, or perhaps in this heat

It is nonsense: the Myth of an Open Road
   Which runs past the orchard gate and beckons
Three brothers in turn to set out over the hills
   And far away, is an invention

Of a climate where it is a pleasure to walk
   And a landscape less populated
Than this one. Even so, to us it looks very odd
   Never to see an only child engrossed

In a game it has made up, a pair of friends
   Making fun in a private lingo,
Or a body sauntering by himself who is not
   Wanting, even as it perplexes

Our ears when cats are called *Cat* and dogs either
   Lupo, Nero or *Bobby*. Their dining
Puts us to shame: we can only envy a people
   So frugal by nature it costs them

No effort not to guzzle and swill. Yet (if I
   Read their faces rightly after ten years)
They are without hope. The Greeks used to call the Sun
   He-who-smites-from-afar, and from here, where

Shadows are dagger-edged, the daily ocean blue,
   I can see what they meant: his unwinking

179

Outrageous eye laughs to scorn any notion
    Of change or escape, and a silent

Ex-volcano, without a stream or a bird,
    Echoes that laugh. This could be a reason
Why they take the silencers off their Vespas,
    Turn their radios up to full volume,

And a minim saint can expect rockets—noise
    As a counter-magic, a way of saying
Boo to the Three Sisters: 'Mortal we may be,
    But we are still here!'—might cause them to hanker

After proximities—in streets packed solid
    With human flesh, their souls feel immune
To all metaphysical threats. We are rather shocked,
    But we need shocking: to accept space, to own

That surfaces need not be superficial
    Nor gestures vulgar, cannot really
Be taught within earshot of running water
    Or in sight of a cloud. As pupils

We are not bad, but hopeless as tutors: Goethe,
    Tapping homeric hexameters
On the shoulder-blade of a Roman girl, is
    (I wish it were someone else) the figure

Of all our stamp: no doubt he treated her well,
    But one would draw the line at calling
The Helena begotten on that occasion,
    Queen of his Second *Walpurgisnacht,*

Her baby: between those who mean by a life a
    Bildungsroman and those to whom living
Means to-be-visible-now, there yawns a gulf
    Embraces cannot bridge. If we try

To 'go southern', we spoil in no time, we grow
   Flabby, dingily lecherous, and
Forget to pay bills: that no one has heard of them
   Taking the Pledge or turning to Yoga

Is a comforting thought—in that case, for all
   The spiritual loot we tuck away,
We do them no harm—and entitles us, I think
   To one little scream at *A piacere*,

Not two. Go I must, but I go grateful (even
   To a certain *Monte*) and invoking
My sacred meridian names, *Vico, Verga,*
   Pirandello, Bernini, Bellini,

To bless this region, its vendanges, and those
   Who call it home: though one cannot always
Remember exactly why one has been happy,
   There is no forgetting that one was.

PROLOGUE:
THE BIRTH OF ARCHITECTURE

FOR JOHN BAYLEY

From gallery-grave and the hunt of a wren-king
   to Low Mass and trailer camp
is hardly a tick by the carbon clock, but I
   don't count that way nor do you:
already it is millions of heartbeats ago
   back to the Bicycle Age,
before which is no *After* for me to measure,

just a still prehistoric *Once*
where anything could happen. To you, to me,
   Stonehenge and Chartres Cathedral,
the Acropolis, Blenheim, the Albert Memorial
   are works by the same Old Man
under different names: we know what He did,
   what, even, He thought He thought,
but we don't see why. (To get that, one would have
   to be selfish in His way,
without concrete or grapefruit.) It's our turn now
   to puzzle the unborn. No world
wears as well as it should but, mortal or not,
   a world has still to be built
because of what we can see from our windows,
   that Immortal Commonwealth
which is there regardless: It's in perfect taste
   and it's never boring but
it won't quite do. Among its populations
   are masons and carpenters
who build the most exquisite shelters and safes,
   but no architects, any more
than there are heretics or bounders: to take
   umbrage at death, to construct
a second nature of tomb and temple, lives
   must know the meaning of *If*.

THANKSGIVING FOR A HABITAT

FOR GEOFFREY GORER

Nobody I know would like to be buried
   with a silver cocktail shaker,
a transistor radio and a strangled
   daily help, or keep his word because

of a great-great-grandmother who got laid
   by a sacred beast. Only a press lord
could have built San Simeon: no unearned income
   can buy us back the gait and gestures

to manage a baroque staircase, or the art
   of believing footmen don't hear
human speech. (In adulterine castles
   our half-strong might hang their jackets

while mending their lethal bicycle chains:
   luckily, there are not enough
crags to go round.) Still, Hetty Pegler's Tump
   is worth a visit, so is Schönbrunn,

to look at someone's idea of the body
   that should have been his, as the flesh
Mum formulated shouldn't: that whatever
   he does or feels in the mood for,

stocktaking, horseplay, worship, making love,
   he stays the same shape, disgraces
a Royal I. To be overadmired is not
   good enough: although a fine figure

is rare in either sex, others like it
   have existed before. One may
be a Proustian snob or a sound Jacksonian
   democrat, but which of us wants

to be touched inadvertently, even
    by his beloved? We know all about graphs
and Darwin, enormous rooms no longer
    superhumanize, but earnest

city planners are mistaken: a pen
    for a rational animal
is no fitting habitat for Adam's
    sovereign clone. I, a transplant

from overseas, at last am dominant
    over three acres and a blooming
conurbation of country lives, few of whom
    I shall ever meet, and with fewer

converse. Linnaeus recoiled from the Amphibia
    as a naked gruesome rabble,
Arachnids give me the shudders, but fools
    who deface their emblem of guilt

are germane to Hitler: the race of spiders
    shall be allowed their webs. I should like
to be to my water-brethren as a spell
    of fine weather: Many are stupid,

and some, maybe, are heartless, but who is not
    vulnerable, easy to scare,
and jealous of his privacy? (I am glad
    the blackbird, for instance, cannot

tell if I'm talking English, German or
    just typewriting: that what he utters
I may enjoy as an alien rigmarole.) I ought
    to outlast the limber dragonflies

as the muscle-bound firs are certainly
    going to outlast me: I shall not end
down any esophagus, though I may succumb
    to a filter-passing predator,

shall, anyhow, stop eating, surrender my smidge
   of nitrogen to the World Fund
with a drawn-out *Oh* (unless at the nod
   of some jittery commander

I be translated in a nano-second
   to a c.c. of poisonous nothing
in a giga-death). Should conventional
   blunderbuss war and its routiers

invest my bailiwick, I shall of course
   assume the submissive posture:
but men are not wolves and it probably
   won't help. Territory, status,

and love, sing all the birds, are what matter:
   what I dared not hope or fight for
is, in my fifties, mine, a toft-and-croft
   where I needn't, ever, be at home *to*

those I am not at home *with*, not a cradle,
   a magic Eden without clocks,
and not a windowless grave, but a place
   I may go both in and out of.

THE CAVE OF MAKING

IN MEMORIAM LOUIS MACNEICE

For this and for all enclosures like it the archetype
  is Weland's Stithy, an antre
more private than a bedroom even, for neither lovers nor
  maids are welcome, but without a
bedroom's secrets: from the Olivetti portable,
  the dictionaries (the very
best money can buy), the heaps of paper, it is evident
  what must go on. Devoid of
flowers and family photographs, all is subordinate
  here to a function, designed to
discourage daydreams—hence windows averted from
  plausible videnda but admitting a light one
could mend a watch by—and to sharpen hearing: reached
  by an outside staircase, domestic
noises and odors, the vast background of natural
  life are shut off. Here silence
is turned into objects.

                I wish, Louis, I could have shown it you
  while you were still in public,
and the house and garden: lover of women and Donegal,
  from your perspective you'd notice
sights I overlook, and in turn take a scholar's interest
  in facts I could tell you (for instance,
four miles to our east, at a wood palisade, Carolingian
  Bavaria stopped, beyond it
unknowable nomads). Friends we became by personal
  choice, but fate had already
made us neighbors. For Grammar we both inherited
  good mongrel barbarian English
which never completely succumbed to the Roman rhetoric
  or the Roman gravity, that nonsense
which stood none. Though neither of our dads, like Horace's
  wiped his nose on his forearm,
neither was porphyry-born, and our ancestors probably

were among those plentiful subjects
it cost less money to murder. Born so, both of us
    became self-conscious at a moment
when locomotives were named after knights in Malory,
    Science to school boys was known as
Stinks, and the Manor still was politically numinous:
    both watched with mixed feelings
the sack of Silence, the churches empty, the cavalry
    go, the Cosmic Model
become German, and any faith if we had it, in immanent
    virtue died. More than ever
life-out-there is goodly, miraculous, lovable,
    but we shan't, not since Stalin and Hitler,
trust ourselves ever again: we know that, subjectively,
    all is possible.
                    To you, though,
ever since, last Fall, you quietly slipped out of Granusion,
    our moist garden, into
the Country of Unconcern, no possibility
    matters. I wish you hadn't
caught that cold, but the dead we miss are easier
    to talk to: with those no longer
tensed by problems one cannot feel shy and, anyway,
    when playing cards or drinking
or pulling faces are out of the question, what else is there
    to do but talk to the voices
of conscience they have become? From now on, as a visitor
    who needn't be met at the station,
your influence is welcome at any hour in my ubity,
    especially here, where titles
from *Poems* to *The Burning Perch* offer proof positive
    of the maker you were, with whom I
once collaborated, once at a weird Symposium
    exchanged winks as a juggins
went on about Alienation.
                        Who would, for preference,
    be a bard in an oral culture,

obliged at drunken feasts to improvise a eulogy
    of some beefy illiterate burner,
giver of rings, or depend for bread on the moods of a
    Baroque Prince, expected,
like his dwarf, to amuse? After all, it's rather a privilege
    amid the affluent traffic
to serve this unpopular art which cannot be turned into
    background noise for study
or hung as a status trophy by rising executives,
    cannot be "done" like Venice
or abridged like Tolstoy, but stubbornly still insists upon
    being read or ignored: our handful
of clients at least can rune. (It's heartless to forget about
    the underdeveloped countries,
but a starving ear is as deaf as a suburban optimist's:
    to stomachs only the Hindu
integers truthfully speak.) Our forerunners might envy us
    our remnant still able to listen:
as Nietzsche said they would, the *plebs* have got steadily
    denser, the *optimates,*
quicker still on the uptake. (Today, even Talleyrand
    might seem a naïf: he had so
little to cope with.) I should like to become, if possible,
    a minor atlantic Goethe,
with his passion for weather and stones but without his
    silliness re the Cross: at times a bore, but,
while knowing Speech can at best, a shadow echoing
    the silent light, bear witness
to the Truth it is not, he wished it were, as the Francophile
    gaggle of pure songsters
are too vain to. We're no musicians: to stink of Poetry
    is unbecoming, and never
to be dull shows a lack of taste. Even a limerick
    ought to be something a man of
honor, awaiting death from cancer or a firing squad,
    could read without contempt: (at
that frontier I wouldn't dare speak to anyone

in either a prophet's bellow
or a diplomat's whisper).

Seeing you know our mystery
from the inside and therefore
how much, in our lonely dens, we need the companionship
of our good dead, to give us
comfort on dowly days when the self is nonentity
dumped on a mound of nothing,
to break the spell of our self-enchantment when lip-smacking
imps of mawk and hooey
write with us what they will, you won't think me imposing if
I ask you to stay at my elbow
until cocktail time: dear Shade, for your elegy
I should have been able to manage
something more like you than this egocentric monologue,
but accept it for friendship's sake.

DOWN THERE

FOR IRVING WEISS

A cellar underneath the house, though not lived in,
Reminds our warm and windowed quarters upstairs that
Caves water-scooped from limestone were our first dwellings,
A providential shelter when the Great Cold came,
Which woke our feel for somewhere fixed to come back to,
A hole by occupation made to smell human.

Self-walled, we sleep aloft, but still, at safe anchor,
Ride there on caves; lamplit we dine at street level:
But, deep in Mother Earth, beneath her key-cold cloak,

Where light and heat can never spoil what sun ripened,
In barrels, bottles, jars, we mew her kind commons,
Wine, beer, conserves and pickles, good at all seasons.

Encrust with years of clammy grime, the lair, maybe,
Of creepy-crawlies or a ghost, its flagstoned vault
Is not for girls: sometimes, to test their male courage,
A father sends the younger boys to fetch something
For Mother from down there; ashamed to whimper, hearts
     pounding,
They dare the dank steps, re-emerge with proud faces.

The rooms we talk and work in always look injured
When trunks are being packed, and when, without warning,
We drive up in the dark, unlock and switch lights on,
They seem put out: a cellar never takes umbrage;
It takes us as we are, explorers, homebodies,
Who seldom visit others when we don't need them.

UP THERE

FOR ANNE WEISS

Men would never have come to need an attic.
Keen collectors of glass or Roman coins build
Special cabinets for them, dote on, index
Each new specimen: only women cling to
Items out of their past they have no use for,
Can't name now what they couldn't bear to part with.

Up there, under the eaves, in bulging boxes,
Hats, veils, ribbons, galoshes, programs, letters
Wait unworshiped (a starving spider spins for
The occasional fly) : no clock recalls it
Once an hour to the household it's a part of,
No Saint's Day is devoted to its function.

All it knows of a changing world it has to
Guess from children, who conjure in its plenum,
Now an eyrie for two excited sisters,
Where, when Mother is bad, her rage can't reach them,
Now a schooner on which a lonely only
Boy sails north or approaches coral islands.

THE GEOGRAPHY OF THE HOUSE

FOR CHRISTOPHER ISHERWOOD

Seated after breakfast
In this white-tiled cabin
Arabs call *the House where*
    Everybody goes,
Even melancholics
Raise a cheer to Mrs.
Nature for the primal
    Pleasures She bestows.

Sex is but a dream to
Seventy-and-over,
But a joy proposed un-
   -til we start to shave:
Mouth-delight depends on

Virtue in the cook, but
This She guarantees from
	Cradle unto grave.

Lifted off the potty,
Infants from their mothers
Hear their first impartial
	Words of worldly praise:
Hence, to start the morning
With a satisfactory
Dump is a good omen
	All our adult days.

Revelation came to
Luther in a privy
(Crosswords have been solved there)
	Rodin was no fool
When he cast his Thinker,
Cogitating deeply,
Crouched in the position
	Of a man at stool.

All the Arts derive from
This ur-act of making,
Private to the artist:
	Makers' lives are spent
Striving in their chosen
Medium to produce a
De-narcissus-ized en-
	-during excrement.

Freud did not invent the
Constipated miser:
Banks have letter boxes
	Built in their façade,
Marked *For Night Deposits,*
Stocks are firm or liquid,

Currencies of nations
    Either soft or hard.

Global Mother, keep our
Bowels of compassion
Open through our lifetime,
    Purge our minds as well:
Grant us a kind ending,
Not a second childhood,
Petulant, weak-sphinctered,
    In a cheap hotel.

Keep us in our station:
When we get pound-noteish,
When we seem about to
    Take up Higher Thought,
Send us some deflating
Image like the pained ex-
-pression on a Major
    Prophet taken short.

(Orthodoxy ought to
Bless our modern plumbing:
Swift and St. Augustine
    Lived in centuries,
When a stench of sewage
Ever in the nostrils
Made a strong debating
    Point for Manichees.)

Mind and Body run on
Different timetables:
Not until our morning
    Visit here can we
Leave the dead concerns of
Yesterday behind us,
Face with all our courage
    What is now to be.

ENCOMIUM BALNEI

FOR NEIL LITTLE

it is odd that the English
    should have invented the slogan
                a rather dirty people
Cleanliness is next to Godliness
                meaning by that
    a gentleman smells faintly of tar
persuaded themselves that constant cold hydropathy
    would make the sons of gentlemen
pure in heart
         (not that papa or his chilblained offspring can
    hope to be gentry)
            still John Bull's
hip-bath it was
        that made one carnal pleasure lawful
    for the first time since we quarreled
over Faith and Works
           (Shakespeare probably stank
                    Le Grand
    Monarque certainly did)
             thanks to him
shrines where a subarctic fire-cult could meet and marry
    a river-cult from torrid Greece
rose again
        resweetened the hirsute West
                a Roman though
    bath addict
        amphitheater fan
would be puzzled
        seeing the caracallan acreage
    compressed into such a few square feet
mistake them for hideouts
           warrens of some outlawed sect
    who mortify their flesh with strange
implements

he is not that wrong
                    if the tepidarium's
barrel vaulting has migrated
to churches and railroad stations
                        if we no longer
go there to wrestle or gossip
or make love
            (you cannot purchase a conjugal tub)
St. Anthony and his wild brethren
(for them ablutions were tabu
                        a habit of that doomed
behavioral sink this world)
                        have been
just as he thought
                at work
                    we are no more chaste
                                obedient
nor
    if we can possibly help it
poor than he was but
                    enthusiasts who were have taught us.
(besides showing lovers of nature
how to carry binoculars instead of a gun)
the unclassical wonder of being
all by oneself
                though our dwellings may still have a master
who owns the front-door key
                        a bathroom
has only an inside lock
                    belongs today to whoever
is taking a bath
                among us
to withdraw from the tribe at will
                        be neither Parent
Spouse nor Guest
                is a sacrosanct
political right

195

where else shall the Average Ego
find its peace
not in sleep surely
the several worlds we invent as quite as pugnacious
as the one into which we are born
and even more public
on Oxford Street or Broadway
I may escape notice
but never
on roads I dream of
what Eden is there for the lapsed
but hot water
snug in its caul
widows
orphans
exiles may feel as self-important
as an only child
and a sage
be silly without shame
present a Lieder Abend
to a captive audience of his toes
retreat from rhyme and reason into some mallarmesque
syllabic fog
for half an hour
it is wise to forget the time
our daily peril
and each other
good for the soul
once in the twenty-four hour cycle of her body
whether according to our schedule
as we sit down to breakfast
or stand up to welcome
folk for dinner
to feel as if
the Pilgrim's Way
or as some choose to call it
the War Path

were now a square in the Holy City
that what was wrong has been put right

                                    as if Von Hügel's
    hoggers and lumpers were extinct
thinking the same as thanking

                                all military hardware
    already slighted and submerged

GRUB FIRST, THEN ETHICS (Brecht)

FOR MARGARET GARDINER

    Should the shade of Plato
        visit us, anxious to know
    how *anthropos* is, we could say to him: "Well,
        we can read to ourselves, our use
of holy numbers would shock you, and a poet
        may lament—where is Telford
whose bridged canals are still a Shropshire glory,
        where Muir who on a Douglas spruce
rode out a storm and called an earthquake noble,
        where Mr. Vynyian Board,
thanks to whose lifelong fuss the hunted whale now suffers
        a quicker death?—without being
called an idiot, though none of them bore arms or
        made a public splash," then "Look!"
    we would point, for a dig at Athens, "Here
        is the place where we cook."

Though built in Lower Austria,
do-it-yourself America
prophetically blueprinted this
palace kitchen for kingdoms
where royalty would be incognito, for an age when
Courtesy might think: "From your voice
and the back of your neck I know we shall get on
but cannot tell from your thumbs
who is to give the orders." The right note is harder
to hear than in the Age of Poise
when She talked shamelessly to her maid and sang
noble lies with Him, but struck
it can be still in New Cnossos where if I am
banned by a shrug it is my fault,
not Father's, as it is my taste whom
I put below the salt.

The prehistoric hearthstone,
round as a birthday-button
and sacred to Granny, is as old
stuff as the bowel-loosening
nasal war cry, but this all-electric room
where ghosts would feel uneasy,
a witch at a loss, is numinous and again
the center of a dwelling
not, as lately it was, an abhorrent dungeon
where the warm unlaundered meiny
belched their comic prose and from a dream of which
chaste Milady awoke blushing.
House-proud, deploring labor, extolling work,
these engines politely insist
that banausics can be liberals,
a cook a pure artist

who moves everyman
at a deeper level than
Mozart, for the subject of the verb

to-hunger is never a name:
dear Adam and Eve had different bottoms,
    but the neotene who marches
upright and can subtract reveals a belly
    like the serpent's with the same
vulnerable look. Jew, Gentile or pigmy,
    he must get his calories
before he can consider her profile or
    his own, attack you or play chess,
and take what there is however hard to get down:
    then surely those in whose creed
  God is edible may call a fine
    omelette a Christian deed.

    The sin of Gluttony
    is ranked among the Deadly
  Seven, but in murder mysteries
    one can be sure the gourmet
didn't do it: children, brave warriors out of a job,
    can weigh pounds more than they should
and one can dislike having to kiss them yet,
    compared with the thin-lipped, they
are seldom detestable. Some waiter grieves
    for the worst dead bore to be a good
trencherman, and no wonder chefs mature into
    choleric types, doomed to observe
Beauty peck at a master-dish, their one reward
    to behold the mutually hostile
  mouth and eyes of a sinner married
    at the first bite by a smile.

    The houses of our City
    are real enough but they lie
  haphazardly scattered over the earth,
    and her vagabond forum
is any space where two of us happen to meet
    who can spot a citizen

without papers. So, too, can her foes. Where the
    power lies remains to be seen,
the force, though, is clearly with them: perhaps only
    by falling can She become
Her own vision, but we have sworn under four eyes
    to keep Her up—all we ask for,
should the night come when comets blaze and meres break,
    is a good dinner, that we
  may march in high fettle, left foot first,
    to hold her Thermopylae.

FOR FRIENDS ONLY

FOR JOHN AND TECKLA CLARK

Ours yet not ours, being set apart
As a shrine to friendship,
Empty and silent most of the year,
This room awaits from you
What you alone, as visitor, can bring,
A weekend of personal life.

In a house backed by orderly woods,
Facing a tractored sugar-beet country,
Your working hosts engaged to their stint,
You are unlike to encounter
Dragons or romance: were drama a craving,
You would not have come.

Books we do have for almost any
Literate mood, and notepaper, envelopes,
For a writing one (to "borrow" stamps
Is a mark of ill-breeding):

200

Between lunch and tea, perhaps a drive;
After dinner, music or gossip.

Should you have troubles (pets will die,
Lovers are always behaving badly)
And confession helps, we will hear it,
Examine and give our counsel:
If to mention them hurts too much,
We shall not be nosey.

Easy at first, the language of friendship
Is, as we soon discover,
Very difficult to speak well, a tongue
With no cognates, no resemblance
To the galimatias of nursery and bedroom,
Court rhyme or shepherd's prose,

And, unless often spoken, soon goes rusty.
Distance and duties divide us,
But absence will not seem an evil
If it make our re-meeting
A real occasion. Come when you can:
Your room will be ready.

In Tum-Tum's reign a tin of biscuits
On the bedside table provided
For nocturnal munching. Now weapons have changed,
And the fashion in appetites:
There, for sunbathers who count their calories,
A bottle of mineral water.

Felicissima notte! May you fall at once
Into a cordial dream, assured
That whoever slept in this bed before
Was also someone we like,
That within the circle of our affection
Also you have no double.

TONIGHT AT SEVEN-THIRTY

FOR M. F. K. FISHER

     The life of plants
  is one continuous solitary meal,
      and ruminants
hardly interrupt theirs to sleep or to mate, but most
      predators feel
ravenous most of the time and competitive
always, bolting such morsels as they can contrive
to snatch from the more terrified: pack-hunters do
     dine *en famille,* it is true,
with protocol and placement, but none of them play host
  to a stranger whom they help first. Only man,
     supererogatory beast,
  Dame Kind's thoroughbred lunatic, can
      do the honors of a feast,

     and was doing so
  before the last Glaciation when he offered
      mammoth-marrow
and, perhaps, Long Pig, will continue till Doomsday
      when at God's board
the saints chew pickled Leviathan. In this age farms
are no longer crenellated, only cops port arms,
but the Law of the Hearth is unchanged: a brawler may not
     be put to death on the spot,
but he is asked to quit the sacral dining area
  instanter, and a foul-mouth gets the cold
     shoulder. The right of a guest
to standing and foster is as old
     as the ban on incest.

     For authentic
comity the gathering should be small
     and unpublic:
at mass banquets where flosculent speeches are made

in some hired hall
we think of ourselves or nothing. Christ's cenacle
seated a baker's dozen, King Arthur's rundle
the same, but today, when one's host may well be his own
     chef, servitor and scullion,
when the cost of space can double in a decade,
   even that holy Zodiac number is
      too large a frequency for us:
   in fact, six lenient semble sieges,
         none of them perilous,

      is now a Perfect
   Social Number. But a dinner party,
         however select,
is a worldly rite that nicknames or endearments
      or family
diminutives would profane: two doters who wish
to tiddle and curmurr between the soup and fish
belong in restaurants, all children should be fed
      earlier and be safely in bed.
Well-liking, though, is a must: married maltalents
   engaged in some covert contrast can spoil
      an evening like the glance
   of a single failure in the toil
         of his bosom grievance.

      Not that a god,
   immune to grief, would be an ideal guest:
         he would be too odd
to talk to and, despite his imposing presence, a bore,
         for the funniest
mortals and the kindest are those who are most aware
of the baffle of being, don't kid themselves our care
is consolable, but believe a laugh is less
      heartless than tears, that a hostess
prefers it. Brains evolved after bowels, therefore,
   great assets as fine raiment and good looks
      can be on festive occasions,

they are not essential like artful cooks
    and stalwart digestions.

I see a table
  at which the youngest and oldest present
    keep the eye grateful
for what Nature's bounty and grace of Spirit can create:
    for the ear's content
one raconteur, one gnostic with amazing shop,
both in a talkative mood but knowing when to stop,
and one wide-traveled worldling to interject now and then
    a sardonic comment, men
and women who enjoy the cloop of corks, appreciate
  depatical fare, yet can see in swallowing
    a sign act of reverence,
  in speech a work of re-presenting
    the true olamic silence.

THE CAVE OF NAKEDNESS

FOR LOUIS AND EMMIE KRONENBERGER

Don Juan needs no bed, being far too impatient to undress,
nor do Tristan and Isolda, much too in love to care
  for so mundane a matter, but unmythical
mortals require one, and prefer to take their clothes off,
  if only to sleep. That is why bedroom farces
must be incredible to be funny, why Peeping Toms
  are never praised, like novelists or bird watchers,
for their keenness of observation: where there's a bed,
  be it a nun's restricted cot or an Emperor's
baldachined and nightly-redamselled couch, there are no
  effable data. (Dreams may be repeatable,
but our deeds of errantry in the wilderness of wish

so often turn out, when told, to be less romantic
than our day's routine: besides, we cannot describe them
    without faking.) Lovers don't see their embraces
as a viable theme for debate, nor a monk his prayers
    (do they, in fact, remember them?): O's of passion,
interior acts of attention, not being a story
    in which the names don't matter but the way of telling,
with a lawyer's wit or a nobleman's assurance,
    does, need a drawing room of their own. Bed-sitting-rooms
soon drive us crazy, a dormitory even sooner
    turns us to brutes: bona fide architects know
that doors are not emphatic enough, and interpose,
    as a march between two realms, so alien, so disjunct,
the no-man's-land of a stair. The switch from personage,
    with a state number, a first and family name,
to the naked Adam or Eve, and vice versa,
    should not be off-hand or abrupt: a stair retards it
to a solemn procession.

                          Since my infantile entrance
    at my mother's bidding into Edwardian England,
I have suffered the transit over forty thousand times,
    usually, to my chagrin, by myself: about
blended flesh, those midnight colloquia of Derbies and Joans,
    I know nothing therefore, about certain occult
antipathies perhaps too much. Some perks belong, though
    to all unwilling celibates: our rooms are seldom
battlefields, we enjoy the pleasure of reading in bed
    (as we grow older, it's true, we may find it prudent
to get nodding drunk first), we retain the right to choose
    our sacred image. (That I often start with sundry
splendors at sundry times greened after, but always end
    aware of one, the same one, may be of no importance,
but I hope it is.) Ordinary human unhappiness
    is life in its natural color, to cavil
putting on airs: at day-wester to think of nothing
    benign to memorize is as rare as feeling
no personal blemish, and Age, despite its damage,

is well-off. When they look in their bedroom mirrors,
Fifty-plus may be bored, but Seventeen is faced by
    a frowning failure, with no money, no mistress,
no manner of his own, who never got to Italy
    nor met a great one: to say a few words at banquets,
to attend a cocktail party in honor of N or M,
    can be severe, but Junior has daily to cope
with ghastly family meals, with dear Papa and Mama
    being odd in the wrong way. (It annoys him to speak,
and it hurts him not to.)
                        When I disband from the world,
    and entrust my future to the Gospel Makers,
I need not fear (not in neutral Austria) being called for
    in the waist of the night by deaf agents, never
to be heard of on earth again: the assaults I would be spared
    are none of them princely—fire, nightmare, insomnia's
Vision of Hell, when Nature's wholesome genial fabric
    lies utterly discussed and from a sullen vague
wafts a contagious stench, her adamant minerals
    all corrupt, each life a worthless iteration
of the general loathing (to know that, probably,
    its cause is chemical can degrade the panic,
not stint it). As a rule, with pills to help them, the Holy Four
    exempt my nights from nuisance, and even wake me
when I would be woken, when, audible here and there
    in the half-dark, members of an avian orchestra
are already softly noodling, limbering up for
    an overture at sunrise, their effort to express
in the old convention they inherit that joy in beginning
    for which our species was created, and declare it
good.
        We may not be obliged—though it is mannerly—to bless
    the Trinity that we are corporal contraptions,
but only a villain will omit to thank Our Lady or
    her henwife, Dame Kind, as he, she, or both ensemble,
emerge from a private cavity to be reborn,
    reneighbored in the Country of Consideration.

THE COMMON LIFE

FOR CHESTER KALLMAN

A living room, the catholic area you
    (Thou, rather) and I may enter
without knocking, leave without a bow, confronts
    each visitor with a style,

a secular faith: he compares its dogmas
    with his, and decides whether
he would like to see more of us. (Spotless rooms
    where nothing's left lying about

chill me, so do cups used for ashtrays or smeared
    with lipstick: the homes I warm to,
though seldom wealthy, always convey a feeling
    of bills being promptly settled

with checks that don't bounce.) There's no *We* at an instant,
    only *Thou* and *I,* two regions
of protestant being which nowhere overlap:
    a room is too small, therefore,

if its occupants cannot forget at will
    that they are not alone, too big
if it gives them any excuse in a quarrel
    for raising their voices. What,

quizzing ours, would Sherlock Holmes infer? Plainly,
    ours is a sitting culture
in a generation which prefers comfort
    (or is forced to prefer it)

to command, would rather incline its buttocks
    on a well-upholstered chair
than the burly back of a slave: a quick glance
    at book titles would tell him

that we belong to the clerisy and spend much
   on our food. But could he read
what our prayers and jokes are about, what creatures
   frighten us most, or what names

head our roll call of persons we would least like
   to go to bed with? What draws
singular lives together in the first place,
   loneliness, lust, ambition,

or mere convenience, is obvious, why they drop
   or murder one another
clear enough: how they create, though, a common world
   between them, like Bombelli's

impossible yet useful numbers, no one
   has yet explained. Still, they do
manage to forgive impossible behavior,
   to endure by some miracle

conversational tics and larval habits
   without wincing (were you to die,
I should miss yours). It's a wonder that neither
   has been butchered by accident,

or, as lots have, silently vanished into
   History's criminal noise
unmourned for, but that, after twenty-four years,
   we should sit here in Austria

as cater-cousins, under the glassy look
   of a Naples Bambino,
the portrayed regards of Strauss and Stravinsky,
   doing British crossword puzzles,

is very odd indeed. I'm glad the builder gave
   our common-room small windows

through which no observed outsider can observe us:
   every home should be a fortress,

equipped with all the very latest engines
   for keeping Nature at bay,
versed in all ancient magic, the arts of quelling
   the Dark Lord and his hungry

animivorous chimeras. (Any brute
   can buy a machine in a shop,
but the sacred spells are secret to the kind,
   and if power is what we wish

they won't work.) *The ogre will come in any case:*
   so Joyce has warned us. Howbeit,
fasting or feasting, we both know this: without
   the Spirit we die, but life

without the Letter is in the worst of taste,
   and always, though truth and love
can never really differ, when they seem to,
   the subaltern should be truth.

YOU

Really, must you,
Over-familiar
Dense companion,
Be there always?
The bond between us
Is chimerical surely:
Yet I cannot break it.

Must I, born for
Sacred play,
Turn base mechanic
So you may worship
Your secular bread,
With no thought
Of the value of time?

Thus far I have known your
Character only
From its pleasanter side,
But you know I know
A day will come
When you grow savage
And hurt me badly.

Totally stupid?
Would that you were:
But, no, you plague me
With tastes I was fool enough
Once to believe in.
Bah!, blockhead:
I know where you learned them.

Can I trust you even
On creaturely fact?
I suspect strongly

You hold some dogma
Of positive truth,
And feed me fictions:
I shall never prove it.

Oh, I know how you came by
A sinner's cranium,
How between two glaciers
The master-chronometer
Of an innocent primate
Altered its tempi:
That explains nothing.

Who tinkered and why?
Why am I certain,
Whatever your faults are,
The fault is mine,
Why is loneliness not
A chemical discomfort,
Nor Being a smell?

ON THE CIRCUIT

Among pelagian travelers,
Lost on their lewd conceited way
To Massachusetts, Michigan,
Miami or L.A.,

An airborne instrument I sit,
Predestined nightly to fulfill

Columbia-Giesen-Management's
Unfathomable will,

By whose election justified,
I bring my gospel of the Muse
To fundamentalists, to nuns,
To Gentiles and to Jews,

And daily, seven days a week,
Before a local sense has jelled,
From talking-site to talking-site
Am jet-or-prop-propelled.

Though warm my welcome everywhere,
I shift so frequently, so fast,
I cannot now say where I was
The evening before last,

Unless some singular event
Should intervene to save the place,
A truly asinine remark,
A soul-bewitching face,

Or blessed encounter, full of joy,
Unscheduled on the Giesen Plan,
With, here, an addict of Tolkien,
There, a Charles Williams fan.

Since Merit but a dunghill is,
I mount the rostrum unafraid:
Indeed, 'twere damnable to ask
If I am overpaid.

Spirit is willing to repeat
Without a qualm the same old talk,
But Flesh is homesick for our snug
Apartment in New York.

A sulky fifty-six, he finds
A change of mealtime utter hell,
Grown far too crotchety to like
A luxury hotel.

The Bible is a goodly book
I always can peruse with zest,
But really cannot say the same
For Hilton's *Be My Guest,*

Nor bear with equanimity
The radio in students' cars,
Musak at breakfast, or—dear God!—
Girl-organists in bars.

Then, worst of all, the anxious thought,
Each time my plane begins to sink
And the No Smoking sign comes on:
What will there be to drink?

Is this a milieu where I must
How grahamgreeneish! How infra dig!
Snatch from the bottle in my bag
An analeptic swig?

Another morning comes: I see,
Dwindling below me on the plane,
The roofs of one more audience
I shall not see again.

God bless the lot of them, although
I don't remember which was which:
God bless the U.S.A., so large,
So friendly, and so rich.

AFTER READING A CHILD'S GUIDE TO MODERN PHYSICS

If all a top physicist knows
About the Truth be true,
Then, for all the so-and-so's,
Futility and grime,
Our common world contains,
We have a better time
Then the Greater Nebulae do,
Or the atoms in our brains.

Marriage is rarely bliss
But, surely it would be worse
As particles to pelt
At thousands of miles per sec
About a universe
In which a lover's kiss
Would either not be felt
Or break the loved one's neck.

Though the face at which I stare
While shaving it be cruel
For, year after year, it repels
An aging suitor, it has,
Thank God, sufficient mass
To be altogether there,
Not an indeterminate gruel
Which is partly somewhere else.

Our eyes prefer to suppose
That a habitable place
Has a geocentric view,
That architects enclose
A quiet Euclidean space:
Exploded myths—but who
Would feel at home astraddle
An ever expanding saddle?

This passion of our kind
For the process of finding out
Is a fact one can hardly doubt,
But I would rejoice in it more
If I knew more clearly what
We wanted the knowledge for,
Felt certain still that the mind
Is free to know or not.

It has chosen once, it seems,
And whether our concern
For magnitude's extremes
Really become a creature
Who comes in a median size,
Or politicizing Nature
Be altogether wise,
Is something we shall learn.

WHITSUNDAY IN KIRCHSTETTEN

FOR H. A. REINHOLD

Grace dances. I would pipe. Dance ye all.
—Acts of John

 Komm Schöpfer Geist I bellow as Herr Beer
picks up our slim offerings and Pfarrer Lustkandl
 quietly gets on with the Sacrifice
as Rome does it: outside car-worshipers enact
 the ritual exodus from Vienna
their successful cult demands (though reckoning time
 by the Jewish week and the Christian year

like their pedestrian fathers). When Mass is over,
      although obedient to Canterbury,
I shall be well gruss-gotted, asked to contribute
      to *Caritas,* though a metic come home
to lunch on my own land: no doubt, if the Allies had not
      conquered the Ost-Mark, if the dollar fell,
the *Gemütlichkeit* would be less, but when was peace
      or its concomitant smile the worse
for being undeserved?
                              In the onion-tower overhead
      bells blash at the Elevation, calling
on Austria to change: whether the world has improved
      is doubtful, but we believe it could
and the divine Tiberius didn't. Rejoice, the bells
      cry to me. Blake's Old Nobodaddy
in his astronomic telescopic heaven,
      the Big White Christian upstairs, is dead,
and won't come hazing us no more, nor bless our bombs:
      no more need sons of the menalty,
divining their future from plum stones, count aloud
      Army, Navy, Law, Church, nor a Prince
say who is *papabile.* (The Ape of the Living God
      knows how to stage a funeral, though,
as penitents like it: Babel, like Sodom, still
      has plenty to offer, though of course it draws
a better sort of crowd.) Rejoice: we who were born
      congenitally deaf are able
to listen now to rank outsiders. The Holy Ghost
      does not abhor a golfer's jargon,
a Lower-Austrian accent, the cadences even
      of my own little Anglo-American
musico-literary set (though difficult,
      saints at least may think in algebra
without sin): but no sacred nonsense can stand Him.
      Our magic syllables melt away,
our tribal formulae are laid bare: since this morning,
      it is with a vocabulary

216

made wholesomely profane, open in lexicons
  to our foes to translate, that we endeavor
each in his idiom to express the true *magnalia*
  which need no hallowing from us, loaning terms,
exchanging graves and legends. (Maybe, when just now
  Kirchstetten prayed for the dead, only I
remembered Franz Joseph the Unfortunate, who danced
  once in eighty-six years and never
used the telephone.)
                    An altar bell makes a noise
  as the Body of the Second Adam
is shown to some of his torturers, forcing them
  to visualize absent enemies
with the same right to grow hybrid corn and be wicked
  as an Abendlander. As crows fly,
ninety kilometers from here our habits end,
  where minefield and watchtower say NO EXIT
from peace-loving Crimtartary, except for crows
  and agents of peace: from Loipersbach
to the Bering Sea not a living stockbroker,
  and church attendance is frowned upon
like visiting brothels (but the chess and physics
  are still the same). We shall bury you
and dance at the wake, say her chiefs: that, says Reason
  is unlikely. But to most people
I'm the wrong color: it could be the looter's turn
  for latrine duty and the flogging block,
my kin who trousered Africa, carried our smell
  to germless poles.
                    Down a Gothic nave
comes our Pfarrer now, blessing the West with water:
  we may go. There is no Queen's English
in any context for *Geist* or *Esprit*: about
  catastrophe or how to behave in one
What do I know, except what everyone knows—?
  if there when Grace dances, I should dance.

JOSEPH WEINHEBER

(1892–1945)

Reaching my gate, a narrow
lane from the village
passes on into a wood:
when I walk that way
it seems befitting to stop
and look through the fence
of your garden where (under
the circs they had to)
they buried you like a loved
old family dog.

Categorized enemies
twenty years ago,
now next-door neighbors, we might
have become good friends,
sharing a common ambit
and love of the Word,
over a golden *Kremser*
had many a long
language on syntax, commas,
versification.

Yes, yes, it has to be said:
men of great damage
and malengine took you up.
Did they for long, though,
take you in, who to Goebbels'
offer of culture
countered—*in Ruah lossen?*
But Rag, Tag, Bobtail
prefer a stink, and the young
condemn you unread.

What, had you ever heard of
Franz Jägerstätter,
the St. Radegund peasant,
who said his lonely
Nein to the Aryan State
and was beheaded,
would your heart, as Austrian,
poet, have told you?
Good care, of course, was taken
you should hear nothing,

be unprepared for a day
that was bound to come,
a season of dread and tears
and dishevelment
when, transfixed by a nightmare,
you destroyed yourself.
Retribution was ever
a bungler at it:
*dies alles ist furchtbar, hier
nur Schweigen gemäss.*

Unmarked by me, unmourned for,
the hour of your death,
unhailed by you the moment
when, providence-led,
I first beheld Kirchstetten
on a pouring wet
October day in a year
that changed our cosmos,
the *annus mirabilis*
when Parity fell.

Already the realms that lost
were properly warm
and overeating, their crimes
the pedestrian

private sort, those nuisances,
corpses and rubble,
long carted away: for their raped
the shock was fading,
their kidnapped physicists felt
no longer homesick.

Today we smile at weddings
where bride and bridegroom
were both born since the Shadow
lifted, or rather
moved elsewhere: never as yet
has Earth been without
her bad patch, some unplace with
jobs for torturers
(In what bars are they welcome?
What girls marry them?),

or her nutritive surface
at peace all over.
No one, so far as we know,
has ever felt safe:
and so, in secret regions,
good family men
keep eye, devoted as monks,
on apparatus
inside which harmless matter
turns homicidal.

Here, though, I feel as at home
as you did: the same
short-lived creatures re-utter
the same carefree songs,
orchards cling to the regime
they know, from April's
rapid augment of color
till boisterous Fall,

when at each stammering gust
apples thump the ground.

Looking across our valley
where, hidden from view,
Sichelbach tottles westward
to join the Perchling,
humanely modest in scale
and mild in contour,
conscious of grander neighbors
to bow to, mountains
soaring behind me, ahead
a noble river,

I would respect you also,
Neighbor and Colleague,
for even my English ear
gets in your German
the workmanship and the note
of one who was graced
to hear the viols playing
on the impaled green,
committed thereafter *den
Abgrund zu nennen.*

THE HORATIANS

Into what fictive realms can imagination
translate you, Flaccus, and your kin? Not the courts of
     Grand Opera, that *galère*
     of lunatics, power-famished

or love-ravenous, belting out their arias,
nor the wards of *Buffa,* either, where abnormal
    growths of self-love are excised
    by the crude surgery of a

practical joke. Perhaps the only invented
story in which your appearance seems credible
    is the Whodunit: I can
    believe in one of you solving

a murder which has the professionals baffled,
thanks to your knowledge of local topography.
    In our world all of you share
    a love for some particular

place and stretch of country, a farm near Tivoli
or a Radnorshire village: what the Capital
    holds out as a lure, a chance
    to get into Society,

does not tempt you, who wry from crowds, traffic-noises,
bluestockings and millionaires. Your tastes run to
    small dinner parties, small rooms,
    and the tone of voice that suits them,

neither truckle nor thrasonical but softly
certain (a sound wood-winds imitate better
    than strings), your most worldly wish
    a genteel sufficiency of

land or lolly. Among those I really know, the
British branch of the family, how many have
    found in the Anglican Church
    your Maecenas who enabled

a life without cumber, as pastors adjective
to rustic flocks, as organists in trollopish

cathedral towns. Then, in all
labyrinthine economies

there are obscure nooks into which Authority
never pokes a suspicious nose, *embusqué* havens
    for natural bachelors
    and political idiots,

Zoological and Botanical Gardens,
museum basements displaying feudal armor
    or old coins: there, too, we find
    you among the custodians.

Some of you have written poems, usually
short ones, and some kept diaries, seldom published
    till after your deaths, but most
    make no memorable impact

except on your friends and dogs. Enthusiastic
Youth writes you off as cold, who cannot be found on
    barricades, and never shoot
    either yourselves or your lovers.

You thought well of your Odes, Flaccus, and believed they
would live, but knew, and have taught your descendants to
    say with you: "As makers go,
    compared with Pindar or any

of the great foudroyant masters who don't ever
amend, we are, for all our polish, of little
    stature, and, as human lives,
    compared with authentic martyrs

like Regulus, of no account. We can only
do what it seems to us we were made for, look at
    this world with a happy eye
    but from a sober perspective."

SINCE

On a mid-December day,
frying sausages
for myself, I abruptly
felt under fingers
thirty years younger the rim
of a steering wheel,
on my cheek the parching wind
of an August noon,
as passenger beside me
You as then you were.

Slap across a veg-growing
alluvial plain
we raced in clouds of white dust,
and geese fled screaming
as we missed them by inches,
making a beeline
for mountains gradually
enlarging eastward,
joyfully certain nightfall
would occasion joy.

It did. In a flagged kitchen
we were served broiled trout
and a rank cheese: for a while
we talked by the fire,
then, carrying candles, climbed
steep stairs. Love was made
then and there: so halcyoned,
soon we fell asleep
to the sound of a river
swabbling through a gorge.

Since then, other enchantments
have blazed and faded,

enemies changed their address,
and War made ugly
an uncountable number
of unknown neighbors,
precious as us to themselves:
but round your image
there is no fog, and the Earth
can still astonish.

Of what, then, should I complain,
pottering about
a neat suburban kitchen?
Solitude? Rubbish!
It's social enough with real
faces and landscapes
for whose friendly countenance
I at least can learn
to live with obesity
and a little fame.

IN DUE SEASON

Springtime, Summer and Fall: days to behold a world
Antecedent to our knowing, where flowers think
Theirs concretely in scent-colors and beasts, the same
Age all over, pursue dumb horizontal lives
On one level of conduct and so cannot be
Secretary to man's plot to become divine.

Lodged in all is a set metronome: thus, in May
Bird-babes still in the egg click to each other *Hatch!;*
June-struck cuckoos go off-pitch; when obese July
Turns earth's heating up, unknotting their poisoned ropes,
Vipers move into play; warned by October's nip,
Younger leaves to the old give the releasing draught.

Winter, though, has the right tense for a look indoors
At ourselves, and with First Names to sit face-to-face,
Time for reading of thoughts, time for the trying-out
Of new metres and new recipes, proper time
To reflect on events noted in warmer months
Till, transmuted, they take part in a human tale.

There, responding to our cry for intelligence,
Nature's mask is relaxed into a mobile grin,
Stones, old shoes, come alive, born sacramental signs,
Nod to us in the First Person of mysteries
They know nothing about, bearing a message from
The invisible sole Source of specific things.

AUGUST 1968 *— still war in Vietnam*
Horror reigns.

The Ogre does what ogres can,
Deeds quite impossible for Man,
But one prize is beyond his reach,
The Ogre cannot master Speech.
About a subjugated plain,
Among its desperate and slain,
The Ogre stalks with hands on hips,
While drivel gushes from his lips.

RIVER PROFILE

Our body is a moulded river
          —Novalis

Out of a bellicose fore-time, thundering
head-on collisions of cloud and rock in an
up-thrust, crevasse-and-avalanche, troll country,
deadly to breathers,

it whelms into our picture below the melt-line,
where tarns lie frore under frowning cirques, goat-bell,
wind-breaker, fishing-rod, miner's-lamp country,
already at ease with

the mien and gestures that become its kindness,
in streams, still anonymous, still jumpable,
flows as it should through any declining country
in probing spirals.

Soon of a size to be named and the cause of
dirty in-fighting among rival agencies,
down a steep stair, penstock-and-turbine country,
it plunges ram-stam,

to foam through a wriggling gorge incised in softer
strata, hemmed between crags that nauntle heaven,
robber-baron, tow-rope, portage-way country,
nightmare of merchants.

Disemboguing from foothills, now in hushed meanders,
now in riffling braids, it vaunts across a senile
plain, well-entered, chateau-and-cider-press country,
its regal progress

gallanted for a while by quibbling poplars,
then by chimneys: led off to cool and launder
retort, steam-hammer, gasometer country,
it changes color.

Polluted, bridged by girders, banked by concrete,
now it bisects a polyglot metropolis,
ticker-tape, taxi, brothel, foot-lights country,
à-la-mode always.

Broadening or burrowing to the moon's phases,
turbid with pulverized wastemantle, on through
flatter, duller, hotter, cotton-gin country
it scours, approaching

the tidal mark where it puts off majesty,
disintegrates, and through swamps of a delta,
punting-pole, fowling-piece, oyster-tongs country,
wearies to its final

act of surrender, effacement, atonement
in a huge amorphous aggregate, no cuddled
attractive child ever dreams of, non-country,
image of death as

a spherical dew-drop of life. Unlovely
monsters, our tales believe, can be translated
too, even as water, the selfless mother
of all especials.

PROLOGUE AT SIXTY

FOR FRIEDRICH HEER

Dark-green upon distant heights
the stationary flocks foresters tend,
blond and fertile the fields below them:

browing a hogback, an oak stands
post-alone, light-demanding.

Easier to hear, harder to see,
limbed lives, locomotive,
automatic and irritable,
social or solitary, seek their foods,
mates and territories while their time lasts.

Radial republics, rooted to spots,
bilateral monarchies, moving frankly,
stoic by sort and self-policing,
enjoy their rites, their realms of data,
live well by the Law of their Flesh.

All but the youngest of the yawning mammals,
Name-Giver, Ghost-Fearer,
maker of wars and wisecracks,
a rum creature, in a crisis always,
the anxious species to which I belong,

whom chance and my own choice have arrived
to bide here yearly from bud-haze
to leaf-blush, dislodged from elsewhere,
by blood barbarian, in bias of view
a Son of the North, outside the *limes*.

Rapacious pirates my people were,
crude and cruel, but not calculating,
never marched in step nor made straight roads,
nor sank like senators to a slave's taste
for grandiose buildings and gladiators.

But the Gospel reached the unroman lands.
I can translate what onion-towers
of five parish churches preach in Baroque:
to make One, there must be Two,
Love is substantial, all Luck is good,

Flesh must fall through fated time
From birth to death, both unwilled,
but Spirit may climb counterwise
from a death, in faith freely chosen,
to resurrection, a re-beginning.

And the Greek Code got to us also:
a Mind of Honor must acknowledge
the happy eachness of all things,
distinguish even from odd numbers,
and bear witness to what-is-the-case.

East, West, on the Autobahn
motorists whoosh, on the Main Line
a far-sighted express will snake by,
through a gap granted by grace of nature:
still today, as in the Stone Age,

our sandy vale is a valued passage.
Alluvial flats, flooded often,
lands of outwash, lie to the North,
to the South litters of limestone alps
embarrass the progress of path-seekers.

Their thoughts upon ski-slope or theatre-opening,
few who pass us pay attention
to our squandered hamlets where at harvest time
chugging tractors, child-driven,
shamble away down sheltered lanes.

Quiet now but acquainted too
with unwelcome visitors, violation,
scare and scream, the scathe of battle:
Turks have been here, Boney's legions,
Germans, Russians, and no joy they brought.

Though the absence of hedgerows is odd to me
(no Whig landlord, the landscape vaunts,
ever empired on Austrian ground),
this unenglish tract after ten years
into my love has looked itself,

added its names to my numinous map
of the *Solihull* gas-works, gazed at in awe
by a bronchial boy, the *Blue John Mine*,
the *Festiniog* railway, the *Rhayader* dams,
Cross Fell, Keld and *Cauldron Snout*,

of sites made sacred by something read there,
a lunch, a good lay, or sheer lightness of heart,
the *Fürbringer* and the *Friedrich Strasse*,
Isafjördur, Epomeo,
Poprad, Basel, Bar-le-Duc,

of more modern holies, *Middagh Street*,
Carnegie Hall and the *Con-Ed* stacks
on *First Avenue*. Who am I now?
An American? No, a New Yorker,
who opens his *Times* at the obit page,

whose dream images date him already,
awake among lasers, electric brains,
do-it-yourself sex manuals,
bugged phones, sophisticated
weapon-systems and sick jokes.

Already a helpless orbited dog
has blinked at our sorry conceited O,
where many are famished, few look good,
and my day turned out torturers
who read *Rilke* in their rest periods.

Now the Cosmocrats are crashed through time-zones
in jumbo jets to a Joint Conference:

231

nor sleep nor shit have our shepherds had,
and treaties are signed (with secret clauses)
by Heads who are not all there.

Can Sixty make sense to Sixteen-Plus?
What has my camp in common with theirs,
with buttons and beards and Be-Ins?
Much, I hope. In *Acts* it is written
Taste was no problem at Pentecost.

To speak is human because human to listen,
beyond hope, for an Eighth Day,
when the creatured Image shall become the Likeness:
Giver-of-Life, translate for me
till I accomplish my corpse at last.

INDEX OF POEMS

234

INDEX OF FIRST LINES

237

240

ABOUT THE AUTHOR

WYSTAN HUGH AUDEN was born in York, England, in 1907. He has been a resident of the United States since 1939, and an American citizen since 1946. Educated at Gresham's School, Holt, and at Christ Church, Oxford, he became associated with a small group of young writers in London—among them Stephen Spender and Christopher Isherwood. He is the author of several volumes of poetry and essays. Mr. Auden has been the recipient of a number of awards, among them the Pulitzer Prize in Poetry, the Guinness Poetry Award and, in 1967, the National Medal for Literature given by the National Book Committee.

VINTAGE FICTION, POETRY, AND PLAYS

VINTAGE BIOGRAPHY AND AUTOBIOGRAPHY